THE UFO
INVESTIGATOR'S HANDBOOK

THE UFO INVESTIGATOR'S HANDBOOK

THE PRACTICAL GUIDE TO RESEARCHING, IDENTIFYING, AND DOCUMENTING UNEXPLAINED SIGHTINGS

CRAIG GLENDAY

FOREWORD BY
STANTON T. FRIEDMAN

RUNNING PRESS
PHILADELPHIA · LONDON

For Mum and Dad

Text copyright © Craig Glenday 1999
This edition copyright © Eddison Sadd Editions 1999
First published in the United States in 1999 by Running Press Book Publishers
All rights reserved under the Pan-American and International Copyright Conventions
Printed and bound by Nordica International Ltd, China

9 8 7 6 5 4 3 2 1

Digit on the right indicates the number of this printing

Library of Congress Cataloging-in-Publication Number 99-70311

ISBN 0-7624-0619-4

The right of Craig Glenday to be identified as the author of this work has been
asserted in accordance with the British Copyright, Design and Patents Act 1988.

AN EDDISON•SADD EDITION
Edited, designed and produced by
Eddison Sadd Editions Limited
St Chad's House
148 King's Cross Road
London WC1X 9DH UK

Phototypeset in TheMix and using QuarkXpress on Apple Macintosh
Origination by Job Color SRL, Italy

This book may be ordered by mail from the publisher. Please include $2.50 for
postage and handling.

But try your bookstore first!

Running Press Book Publishers
125 South Twenty-second Street
Philadelphia, Pennsylvania 19103-4399

Visit us on the web!
www.runningpress.com

Contents

Foreword

As a nuclear physicist who has had a strong interest in flying saucers since 1958 and has lectured on the controversial topic "Flying Saucers ARE Real!" in fifteen countries, I must read many, many UFO books just to keep up. This handbook is clearly unique, covering some ground that no other book covers. For example, nowhere else have I seen not only the location of UFO hotspots, but how to get there, and where to get information about that area. And there is solid information about the dates of meteor showers and the lighting on aircraft to help an investigator sort out witness observations.

I am often asked, "How can I get started on UFO research?" especially by younger people who come to my lectures, or have seen me on some TV program, or mentioned in a newspaper article, or, most common of all, who have discovered the many sites dealing with UFOs on the Internet. This book will serve as a useful primer for those intrigued with such questions as, "Where can I find out more about abductions or about the radiotelescope-based SETI?" This book is not an encyclopedia about UFOs, of which there are several already. Neither is it a textbook for professors teaching a course about UFOs, though it could certainly be used by those with enough courage to take on such a project. However, it does cover in some depth all its topics of UFO research, from equipment to have on hand when investigating a sighting to questions to ask witnesses, and how to analyze a UFO photograph or video. And what about those contactee stories ...? All told in a breezy, non-pedantic style, it is visually appealing with many illustrations.

Craig Glenday tends to be pretty much middle of the road in all his discussions. I personally know many of the researchers he mentions, and found him to be fair. He raises more questions than he answers, such as about cover-ups by various governments and the role of the CIA. He has sense enough not to go into a detailed examination of either the Roswell Incident or Operation Majestic-12, though he touches on both—and there are certainly many books about Roswell. He seems appropriately skeptical about the Drake equation purporting to tell the number of civilizations in the galaxy. It was good to see a brief discussion of the very important disappearance of a pilot, Frederick Valentich, and his aircraft while flying over the Bass Strait between Tasmania and Australia. Readers will be pleased, I think, to discover cases from many countries. All too many books focus on primarily North American cases.

Having read Glenday's book my enthusiasm is renewed to do a book on the physics aspects of flying saucers, such as methods for interstellar travel, or how much acceleration can be withstood by people. And it will include puzzling questions, such as why aliens might wish to come to planet earth and why governments might want to cover up the facts about this very important subject?

I am sure that those who read this handbook will be stimulated to want to learn more. It is an excellent appetizer to a feast of ufology.

Stanton T. Friedman

UFOs and Generation X

This book is the result of months of constantly being asked 'How do I investigate UFOs?' During my tenure as editor of a popular 'mysteries' magazine series, my team and I were asked this question on an almost daily basis. It seemed that Generation X – the wave of UFO hobbyists brought up on a diet that included *The X Files* – wanted to take their interest in ufology a step beyond simply reading about the latest sightings or classic cases. While there were many books recounting case after case of sightings, contacts, abductions and cover-ups, there was no single, up-to-date book in print to which I could refer readers for information on how to investigate UFOs.

What was needed was a proactive handbook that would present an overview of the entire subject while giving brief guidelines on how to carry out field investigations. Some UFO groups already distribute their own guidelines, but the occasional newsletter just isn't enough for many hobbyists. What they want is to get out there and do it for themselves – or at least have the knowledge to do this, should the need arise.

This was one good reason for writing this handbook. Another was to take UFO investigation out of the hands of so-called professional ufologists and make it available to the enthusiast. Without meaning any disrespect to the genuine researcher, ufology has lined too many pockets, bolstered too many egos, and made too many celebrities out of non-entities...

MAIN PICTURE: *Ufologist keep their eyes on the skies in the hope of catching a glimpse of a UFO. Skywatching – in which investigators camp out in areas of ufological interest – is one of the few ways in which you can participate actively in the UFO phenomenon. This book will hopefully provide you with some more ideas for becoming more proactive ufologist.*

WHAT ISN'T IT ABOUT?

This book is not about where aliens come from, or what their agenda is. It's not about how to see flying saucers or communicate with them. And it's not about arguing the physics of interstellar travel or gossiping about high-level cover-ups. *The UFO Investigator's Handbook* is about recognizing that weird things are seen in the sky and experienced by ordinary people. I'm not saying that aliens do or don't exist. But I do try to help people make sense of these episodes and come to terms with them.

Perhaps most importantly, this book is about enjoying ufology as a hobby. For the amateur, UFO research is one of those rare pastimes that attracts thousands of participants who don't actually take part. At best, you can visit conventions or read books. What I hope I've done is give readers the confidence to investigate for themselves.

Finally, it's worth noting that many significant scientific achievements have

ABOVE: *Philosopher Charles Fort (1874–1932), arguably the father of ufology, strongly criticized science for its dismissive approach to the "unexplained."*

come from amateur and self-taught scientists – the physicist Michael Faraday and the inventor Thomas Edison, for example, are just two of the greatest amateur scientific minds. It's with this audacious sense of scientific achievement that this book is dedicated to the amateur ufologist.

THE NUTS AND BOLTS OF THE BOOK

The book divides into easily digestible units of information, and, because it's not affiliated to any one group or doctrine, covers topics considered by many to be controversial or outmoded, such as hypnotic regression and crop circles. While the inclusion of these subjects may seem to contradict the basic premise of investigating UFOs, they have become an intrinsic part of the phenomenon and deserve study-if, for no other reason, than to rule them out of the equation.

• Chapters 1 to 3 – SIGHTINGS, LANDINGS, AND ENCOUNTERS – cover the investigation of the the four standard "close-encounter" categories

• Chapter 4 – ANALYSIS – deals with the collection and assessment of visual evidence.

• Chapter 5 – RESEARCH – is a guide to investigating government and military involvement in the UFO phenomenon

• Chapter 6 – HOTSPOTS – is an international gazetteer of places of interest to ufologists

What is this thing called ... UFOLOGY?

SO, WHAT EXACTLY ARE WE DEALING WITH HERE? THE ANSWER SHOULD BE FAIRLY SIMPLE – THE INVESTIGATION OF OBJECTS SEEN IN THE SKY THAT CANNOT EASILY BE IDENTIFIED. BUT, OF COURSE, IT'S NOT QUITE THIS STRAIGHTFORWARD ...

Since the term UFO was first coined, researchers have constantly revised the definition, widening the scope as they went:

▶ "Any aerial object which the observer is unable to identify." (US Air Force, 1966)

▶ "The stimulus for a report made by one or more individuals of something seen in the sky (or an object thought to be capable of flight but seen when landed on the Earth) which the observer could not identify as having an ordinary natural origin, and which seemed to him sufficiently puzzling that he undertook to make a report of it to the police, to government officials, to the press, or perhaps to a representative of a private organization devoted to the study of such objects." (University of Colorado UFO Project, 1969)

▶ "A moving aerial or celestial phenomenon, detected visually or by radar, but whose nature is not immediately understood." (Dr. Carl Sagan, 1972)

HUMAN ISSUE

These definitions act as eloquent testimony to the complexity of the UFO phenomenon. However, what most descriptions lack is the fact that ufology is not the study of UFOs – it is actually all about the people who report them. Of course, physical evidence is often presented, but this serves only to support or debunk witness testimony. Ultimately, the main witnesses to a UFO encounter will have sped off in their "spacecraft" long before UFO investigators are contacted. All that usually remains is a very confused, and very human, "UFO experiencer."

UFOLOGY VERSUS SAUCEROLOGY

Over the past fifty years, there has emerged a new branch of ufology concerned with establishing the existence of extraterrestrial craft and their crews. Proponents of this "saucerology" begin with the assumption that alien life forms do exist and that they are visiting our planet.

Whatever your starting point – ufologist or saucerologist – your aim as an investigator is the same: to eliminate those cases that can be explained in terms of natural phenomena, mental anomalies, or man-made objects. Hopefully, this book will help you to do this. It may be necessary for you to seek the assistance of a wide range of professionals – such as astronomers, psychiatrists, photographic analysts, and graphologists – but the use of such professionals can be expensive. Therefore, you have to be sure that the case is strong enough to warrant such expense. Again, the book provides helpful information in this area.

Finally, remember that there is no single answer to the UFO mystery. The fifty frustrating years since Kenneth Arnold's defining sighting have taught us that each case has a unique explanation, and that attempting to account for all cases with a single unifying theory is futile. We must judge each case on its merits, and be prepared to accept the findings, no matter how disappointing or fantastical.

THE FLYING SAUCER STORY

Saucerology began in June 1947 with the claims of Kenneth Arnold (left), a pilot who witnessed a string of nine flying objects over Mount Rainier, Washington State. He reported the UFOs as a five-mile-long formation traveling at a speed far in excess of anything possible in the 1940s.

The history of the UFO goes back much farther than this. Even the term "flying saucer" was 70 years old when it was picked up by the media in 1947 – its first appearance was actually in 1878, when Texas farmer John Martin used it to describe the shape of a dark object "going through space at a wonderful speed." Ironically, when Arnold used the word "saucer," he was describing the objects' motion: "like a saucer would if you skipped it across water." It was East Oregon journalist Bill Bequette who used the phrase to describe their shape, which in turn led the Associated Press news agency to coin the more media-friendly term "flying saucer."

ABOVE: Kenneth Arnold's experience was publicized in the pulp magazine Fate. While popularizing ufology, Fate's mass-market approach set the subject back for years.

RIGHT: Kenneth Arnold published details of his experience in The Coming of the Saucers (1950). In the book, he also tells of his adventures as the first professional ufologist.

Essential field kit

MAKE SURE YOU HAVE A GOOD FIELD KIT, PACKED AND READY TO USE AT SHORT NOTICE. TAILOR IT TO YOUR BUDGET—AND DON'T FORGET GOOD BOOTS AND A MAP OF THE AREA.

1

THE UFO REPORT FORM

At the end of the book you will find a blank UFO sighting report form, covering all the important pieces of anecdotal eyewitness evidence that you need to gather. The first stage of any investigation should be to have a copy of this form, or one like it, completed by UFO witnesses. If necessary, the other side of the sheets can be used for drawings, extended descriptions, or explanations. These sheets will then form the basis of a case file.

The sections and headings on the sighting report form are based on information gleaned from a United States Air Force Academy textbook entitled Introductory Space Science.

2

3

1 MAGNIFYING GLASS *Use to analyze anything that you can't collect and remove for later analysis. If evidence can be taken, seal up in a labeled ziplock bag.*

2 FLASHLIGHT (plus spare batteries and bulb) *Find a flashlight with an added fluorescent tube, which will provide wide, hands-free illumination, useful for investigating trace cases at night.*

3 DICTAPHONE (plus spare batteries and cassettes) *Record witness testimony and, if investigating a trace case, a commentary of what you—and any*

accompanying experts—are doing. Transcribe asap and keep the cassettes (with write-protect tabs broken) filed safely.

4 COMPASS *For added accuracy, add compass directions to any notes. Orienteering compasses with small rulers can be placed next to evidence being photographed to give an indication of the subject's scale. Can also be used for picking up any magnetic effects.*

5 PENKNIFE *A good-sized Swiss Army knife with as many attachments as possible is the ultimate*

field tool. Have a minimum of a sawblade, scissors, and tweezers.

6 **NOTEPAD, PEN, AND PENCIL** *Log witness statements (which you should also tape), make sketches and note details about pictures you're taking.*

7 **CAMERA (including flash unit, spare batteries and film of varying speeds)** *Use to keep a visual record. Make sure you get clean, close-up shots of all evidence, and shoot everything from a number of angles. Photographs of the surrounding area will also*

help, especially in landing or crash cases, where the distant environment may have been altered.

8 **STEEL TAPE MEASURE** *Take accurate measurements of anything relevant. For non-straight measurements, use a fabric tape measure (or a piece of string, which can then be measured with the steel tape).*

9 **BINOCULARS** *To provide you with data about the area around trace cases. May also reveal unnoticed details such as distant objects or buildings that could account for reports of nocturnal lights.*

CHAPTER ONE

Sightings

We are all of us in the gutter, but some
of us are looking at the stars.
OSCAR WILDE, *Lady Windermere's Fan*

Since the days of the earliest civilizations, humans have recorded accounts of visitors from the sky. Cave paintings in the south of France dating back 14,000 years depict disklike objects identical to the classic flying-saucer shape. According to ancient stone tablets discovered in Mesopotamia, the Sumerians—probably the first civilization on Earth—believed that a race of "gods" had visited our planet in order to seed life. The Old Testament talks of visitations from a "chariot of fire" (2 Kings 2:11) and a whirlwind of fire containing golden, manlike beings (Ezekiel 1: 4), and accounts of blazing globes, fiery clouds, and flying boats litter Roman and medieval literature.

IDENTIFYING THE UNIDENTIFIED

But as our knowledge of the universe increases, so too does our understanding of the "unexplained." One-time mysteries such as ball lightning and auroras are no longer explained in terms of the supernatural, but as hard scientific fact.

About ninety percent of UFO reports can now be explained in mundane terms—planets and stars, meteorological phenomena, man-made objects, and hallucinations. UFO investigators must be aware of these possibilities in order to channel their energy into finding out about that tiny but fascinating ten percent slice of the inexplicable.

MAIN PICTURE: *As odd as it sounds, clouds can be reported as UFOs. In particular, lenticular clouds—such as this one photographed by astronomer Wayne S. Holland—are commonly mistaken for flying saucers because of their shape.*

LEFT: *Cave paintings in prehistoric France appear to depict a number of saucerlike objects flying above the heads of humans. The existence of such ancient evidence has led many researchers to speculate that alien visitation has occurred throughout the history of humanity. To academics, this is a particularly twentieth century—and unnecessary—interpretation of already-understood events.*

ABOVE: *Mysterious flying objects dominate the skies in this seventeenth-century woodcut from Basel, Switzerland. Dating from August 1566, the woodcut confirms that unidentified flying objects have been seen and logged from time immemorial. Whether or not they are alien spacecraft is a different matter.*

LEFT: *A flaming chariot descends to Earth in order to carry Ezekiel to heaven. Certain ufologists believe that the religious interpretation of this event was an attempt to explain what was actually an extraterrestrial encounter.*

Being there ... eyewitness reports

STEP ONE IN ANY UFO INVESTIGATION IS TO COLLECT INFORMATION ABOUT THE SIGHTING FROM THE WITNESS. DONE PROPERLY, IT CAN SAVE HOURS OF RESEARCH AND PROVIDE ALL THE INFORMATION NEEDED.

Contrary to what cynics say, UFO reports don't come solely from confidence tricksters or attention-seekers. Most witnesses are genuine and usually publicity-shy, with little understanding of their experience.

DELVING DEEPER

It's up to the UFOlogist to help witnesses find some answers. Investigators must make proper use of the witness, who is usually the only source of evidence in a case—details must be extracted methodically and carefully. Learning to master witness psychology is all-important.

Finally, investigators must be wary of the "experimenter" effect, whereby their own desires and opinions influence how the witness reports their story, or how details are interpreted. The witness must tell their story completely, without interjection by the investigator.

SOME GOLDEN RULES

✔ **ACCURACY** *If the witness provides minute details, ask them: how are they so sure? How did they judge the time of the sighting, or the size, speed, and position of the object? Be wary of witnesses trying to impress you, consciously or subconsciously, with details that are actually guesses.*

✔ **INTERPRETATION** *Make sure the witness tells you exactly what they saw, not their interpretation of it. Compare: "... huge black triangle with lights on each corner" with "... three lights arranged in a triangular formation." In the first account, the witness has filled in the blanks and turned their sighting of three lights into an encounter with a black triangle.*

✔ **BELIEF SYSTEMS** *Assess the scope of your witness's knowledge. Do they have any books on ufology or science fiction? What is their favorite movie? This will give some idea of personality, and reveal whether a witness might embellish events.*

✔ **EXTRANEOUS DETAILS** *If initial written or verbal accounts are delivered with honesty, they will usually include "inconsequential" details such as what a witness had for lunch, or what thoughts entered their minds when they saw the object.*

✔ **SEQUENCE** *Be wary of repetition in subsequent retellings, especially in the sequence of events. This may suggest a "scripting" of events rather than a genuine use of the witness's memory.*

LOGGING THE EYEWITNESS'S ACCOUNT

It's important that you obtain accurate written and verbal first-hand accounts (recorded with no interruptions) of the experience, with any necessary illustrations. If the witness writes to you with their experience, treat this as the primary account. With multiple witnesses, make sure written and verbal statements are provided independently. Then, follow these three steps:

1 Ask the witness to complete a UFO report form (see pages 132–134). Make sure forms are signed, dated, copied, and filed.

2 Assess the accuracy of the information. Cross-check written and verbal statements with the report forms. If possible, visit the sighting area—preferably at the same time of day as the sighting, and also during daylight if the sighting occurred at night. Make sure descriptions of the area match, and look around for objects that could have accounted for the sighting. Interview friends, family, and neighbors for corroboration, if relevant.

3 If there are questions, quiz the witness for clarification. Test them on details, and assess how much the story changes, but don't be aggressive. Use this opportunity to build a rapport, since you may need details of your witness's mental, sexual, and medical history.

A POLYGRAPH NEVER LIES

The lie-detector test is an imperfect means of assessing a witness's reliability. A polygraph machine measures physiological responses—such as heart rate and brain activity—that change under stress, such as when witnesses are lying.

There is a skill to using a polygraph, so if you have access to one, make sure it is operated by a professional. Discuss questions in advance with the operator, who will establish the most appropriate way to phrase them. After a series of control questions to establish a non-stress response, the witness can be interrogated either directly ("Did you see a UFO?") or indirectly ("Was the UFO shaped like a disk or triangle?"). Finally, don't rely on the findings, as certain subjects can limit their stress responses.

LEFT: Former President Jimmy Carter reported a UFO encounter in 1969, and provided details of his experience in a UFO report form for the US investigative group NICAP.

Coming to terms with UFOs

ONCE YOU HAVE YOUR WITNESS'S REPORT, HOW DO YOU MAKE SENSE OF IT? FORTUNATELY, DATA CAN BE CLASSIFIED, HELPING INVESTIGATORS MAKE SENSE OF THEIR FINDINGS AND STANDARDIZING HOW EXPERIENCES ARE REPORTED.

The main UFO classification system now in use was devised by one Dr. J. Allen Hynek. Hynek was the US Air Force's UFO consultant between the 1940s and the 1960s, and founder of the Center for UFO Studies. While other systems have since been devised, Hynek's remains the best known and simplest to use.

The system is divided into two parts: distant sightings (those in which an object is judged to be more than 500 feet from the witness) and close encounters (those which take place when the witness is within 500 feet of the object).

DISTANT SIGHTINGS

NOCTURNAL LIGHTS (NLs): Lights in the night sky, the existence of which cannot be explained in terms of natural or man-made phenomena.

DAYLIGHT DISKS (DDs): Any unusual or unidentifiable objects seen during the day. Despite the name, the objects can be any shape.

RADAR VISUALS (RVs): Corroboration of a report on some kind of scientific instrument, usually a radar screen. Anomalous radar blips—known as "angels"—are common, but RVs are rare.

RIGHT: *A spectacular nocturnal light (NL), the most basic form of UFO sighting. While this image shows a dramatic plume of light, most cases involve small points of light that appear to move across the night sky.*

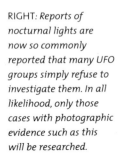

RIGHT: *Reports of nocturnal lights are now so commonly reported that many UFO groups simply refuse to investigate them. In all likelihood, only those cases with photographic evidence such as this will be researched.*

CLOSE ENCOUNTERS

... OF THE FIRST KIND (CEI): Cases in which UFOs come to within 500 feet of a witness but otherwise have no interaction with them or with the environment.

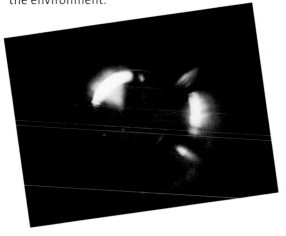

ABOVE: *A close encounter of the first kind. This UFO passed directly over the head of the photographer, who managed to capture the brightly-lit underside of the object.*

... OF THE SECOND KIND (CEII): Cases in which a UFO interacts with the environment and causes physical change, such as scorched earth, frightened or injured animals or humans, and increases in radiation.

... OF THE THIRD KIND (CEIII): UFO events in which nonterrestrial occupants of craft are simply witnessed, without any attempts at contact.

... OF THE FOURTH KIND (CEIV): When a witness experiences trauma suggestive of physical contact with an ET entity. These "reality distortions" include periods of missing time, memory lapses, and post-traumatic stress. There may be physical evidence, such as implants, and physiological change.

... OF THE FIFTH KIND (CEV): This highly controversial class of contact involves witnesses making non-physical contact with an extraterrestrial intelligence—for example, by telepathy. Hynek would, in all likelihood, be most disapproving.

THE HYNEK CONNECTION

*B*etween 1948 and 1969, Dr. J. Allen Hynek, Professor of Astronomy at Northwestern University, served as the US Air Force's scientific consultant for UFO investigations.

Hynek believed that his job was to debunk UFO reports, and for many years he did just that. However, he eventually became convinced that something real was at the heart of the phenomenon. While rejecting the extraterrestrial hypothesis (ETH)—the theory that UFOs are intelligently controlled extraterrestrial craft—he concluded that UFO reports required a much more scientific, empirical investigation.

ABOVE: *J. Allen Hynek, the USAF's UFO adviser, and founder member of the Center for UFO Studies.*

Hynek died in 1986, but not before establishing the Center for UFO Studies and, in doing so, laying the foundations for the respectable and scientific study of UFOs. Part of his invaluable legacy was a classification system for reporting and logging reports of UFO experiences.

Ruling out the routine ... identifying flying objects

MOST UFO REPORTS TURN OUT TO HAVE "LOGICAL" EXPLANATIONS. IS THE REPORT YOU'RE DEALING WITH ONE OF THESE – OR COULD IT BE SOMETHING ELSE?

There is a very real difference between what cannot be explained because there isn't enough data and what cannot be explained simply because the object remains unknown. In cases with insufficient evidence, it is all too easy for the skeptic to choose the most likely mundane explanation.

Donald Menzel, Professor of Astrophysics at Harvard University between 1939 and 1971, believed that most UFO sightings could be explained without the need for the extraterrestrial hypothesis (ETH), and was a vociferous flying-saucer debunker. He went on to devise a list of Identified Flying Objects (IFOs), which he presented at a high-level UFO symposium in December 1969. His tendency was to apply these explanations with enthusiastic abandon to almost every case he investigated. However, if considered objectively, a list such as the one opposite provides a suitable starting point for ruling out the mundane. More details follow over the next few pages.

CHOOSING THE UNKNOWN

All lists, however, come with a caveat: don't force explanations. If an investigation leaves things unresolved, choose the "unknown" conclusion to avoid the *reductio ad absurdum* criticism often leveled at Menzel. I'd like to hear the reactions of airline pilots who've witnessed UFOs and have been told that what they saw was a cigarette butt.

FULL OF HOT AIR

It was a bizarre sight. A glowing, saucer-shaped craft, carrying a silver-suited being, "buzzed" a busy British highway. But this was no space invader – this was Richard Branson. The Virgin entrepreneur was taking part in a publicity stunt for his "Virgin Lightships" – dirigibles bearing advertising – and had his knuckles rapped by police as a result. All eleven Lightships have been involved in cases of mistaken identity across the globe.

OBJECTS OF THE MATERIAL AND IMMATERIAL KIND

1. MATERIAL OBJECTS
- *Meteorological experiments in the ionosphere (such as those with weather balloons)*

- *Planes, military research craft*
- *Barrage balloons/dirigibles*
- *Parachutes, soap bubbles*
- *Clouds, leaves, tumbleweed*
- *Insects, spiders' webs*
- *Flocks of birds*
- *Kites, TV antennae*

- *Fireworks (shown below)*
- *Streetlights*
- *Cigarettes (that have been tossed away while still alight)*
- *Vehicle headlights*

2. IMMATERIAL OBJECTS
- *Auroral phenomena*
- *Noctilucent clouds (certain high-altitude clouds appear to "shine" at night)*
- *Searchlights*
- *Lightning*
- *St. Elmo's Fire (luminous electrical discharges, shown right)*
- *Reflections from fog/mist*
- *Mirages*

3. ASTRONOMICAL PHENOMENA
- *The Moon*
- *Planets, stars*
- *Artificial satellites*
- *Meteors*

4. PHYSIOLOGICAL PHENOMENA
- *After-images from viewing bright objects, such as the Sun, streetlights, and lit matches*
- *Autokinetic illusion – when a bright object against a dark background appears to move erratically. Witnesses making subtle movements without good ambient lighting can give the effect of a distant object moving*

- *Eye defects and Muscae volantes – dead cells or "floaters" in the vitreous humor of the eye.*

5. PSYCHOLOGICAL PHENOMENON
- *Hallucinations and strange sensations, caused by hysteria, dementia, drugs or alcohol, and sleep paralysis*

6. PHOTOGRAPHIC PHENOMENA
(objects appearing in photographs)
- *Double exposures*
- *Development defects*
- *Internal reflections within the camera*

7. RADAR (objects appearing on radar)
- *Unusual refractions*
- *Ghost images*
- *Birds*

8. HOAXES

Up, up in the atmosphere

CLOUDS, ICE CRYSTALS, AURORAS, AND THE LIKE ARE OFTEN MISTAKEN FOR UFOS, SO ANY INVESTIGATOR MUST BECOME FAMILIAR WITH THESE PHENOMENA.

Clyde Tombaugh was no stranger to the sky at night – he had discovered Pluto in 1930, after all. At about 10 o'clock one night, Tombaugh and his wife and mother-in-law were standing on their porch at Las Cruces, New Mexico, admiring what the astronomer described as a "sky of rare transparency." Suddenly, they saw six pale yellow, "windowlike" rectangles pass directly overhead. The lights traveled silently across fifty or sixty degrees of sky within a few seconds, faster than any aircraft could and slower than a meteorite would.

ENTER MENZEL ...

In spite of his fears that reporting the object would jeopardize his reputation as an astronomer, Tombaugh did so, only to face an investigation by arch debunker Donald Menzel. Menzel concluded that what the Tombaughs had seen was in fact the result of a meteorological phenomenon known as temperature inversion, when light from the ground can be reflected off a trapped layer of warm air above the cold night air below it.

RIGHT: *A formation of lights crosses the night sky. But are they aircraft, ground reflections, or a fleet of saucers? If the conditions are right, freak weather phenomena such as temperature inversion can also account for this type of sighting.*

ABOVE: *This amazing lenticular cloud was shot in Hawaii by astronomer Wayne Holland. Despite its flying-saucer shape, few would mistake it for one.*

CLOUDS OF CONTROVERSY

Temperature inversion is just one of many naturally occurring phenomena that enter the UFO debate – there is still a lot we don't know about our atmosphere.

CLOUDS Orographic clouds (formed by the movement of wind around hills) often cause mistaken UFO reports. Lenticular clouds in particular, make very convincing UFOs, in spite of their slow speed and obvious cloud features.

FAR RIGHT AND RIGHT: *Meteorological phenomena such as aurorae (far right) or parhelia (right) are often used to account for UFO reports. In most cases, however, it seems as if debunkers are ignoring the witnesses' descriptions and opting for the easiest answer.*

BALL LIGHTNING Despite the fact that science barely accepts the reality of this freak form of lightning, scientists are happy to offer it as an explanation of UFO sightings.

SUN ANOMALIES Parhelia, also known as "mock suns" or "sundogs," are brightly colored spots of sunlight refracted through hexagonal ice crystals in the air. They are usually seen in pairs, one on each side of the Sun.

MIRAGE On hot days, light distortion caused by heat rising from the ground can cause distant optical illusions.

ST. ELMO'S FIRE/SWAMP GAS Corposants (luminous electrical discharge during electrical storms) and

ABOVE: *Despite eyewitness and photographic evidence, it took the scientific community many years to accept the reality of ball lightning. Will the same be said of the UFO phenomenon?*

ignited swamp gas (methane produced by rotting organic matter) are both sources of unusual bright lights.

Fire in the sky ... earthlights

IS THE ANSWER TO THE UFO PHENOMENON LYING UNDER OUR FEET? COULD UFOS SIMPLY BE BALLS OF IONIZED GAS RELEASED FROM THE EARTH'S CRUST?

Throughout the early 1980s, it appeared as if a remote region of Norway had been chosen as an interstellar meeting point for extraterrestrials. In the farming community of Hessdalen, residents reported being "buzzed" by a series of bizarre lights. Witnesses described encounters with bullet-shaped, cylindrical, and spherical craft. When attempts were made to communicate with the lights using flashlights— a scaled-down version of events in Steven Spielberg's *Close Encounters of the Third Kind*— the "visitors" often complied, flashing back indecipherable answers.

NORWEGIAN HOTSPOT

For a few years, Hessdalen was a UFO hotspot. Dozens of UFOlogists camped out in the freezing countryside and formed Project Hessdalen, monitoring activity around the clock. The Norwegian defense department was even called in and posted two officers to log the bizarre aerial activity.

Then, during 1984, the activity seemed to die away, leaving UFOlogists to ponder the origins of the unusual lights. While many researchers typically looked to the stars for an explanation,

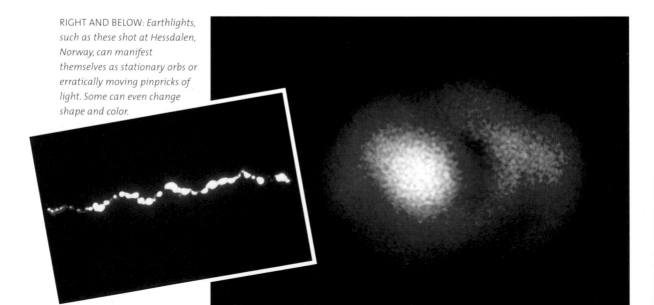

RIGHT AND BELOW: *Earthlights, such as these shot at Hessdalen, Norway, can manifest themselves as stationary orbs or erratically moving pinpricks of light. Some can even change shape and color.*

there was a small band who believed that the way to look was down, literally beneath their feet.

GOING DOWN

Earth-mysteries researchers Paul Devereux and Paul McCartney, and Canadian neuroscientist Dr. Michael Persinger, proposed that the source of the lights at Hessdalen was not another planet but the Earth. Tectonic stress caused by the movement of the Earth's crust, they suggested, was producing strange lights—known as "earthlights" or "balls of light" (BOLs).

French UFOlogist Ferdinand Lagarde was one of the first to correlate UFO sightings and fault lines. The all-important "flying-saucer" sighting by pilot Kenneth Arnold in 1947 took place over the Cascade Mountains, an area prone to geological stress and adjacent to the Yakima Indian Reservation, where researchers have documented a profusion of dancing lights and meteorological phenomena.

STALEMATE

Many UFOlogists oppose this reductionist explanation—it's a huge leap of faith from BOL to intelligently controlled flying saucer. However, when investigating reports of BOLs, it's a good idea to contact a geological society for details of fractures in the area surrounding the sighting (*see pages 135–141*). If you are re-examining an old case, consult these societies for details of geophysical activity about the time of the sightings. If you discover that the location of the UFO is prone to seismic disturbances, there is a chance that the witness encountered an earthlight.

ABDUCTION IN ARIZONA?

Researcher Paul Devereux believes that earthlights can even account for the alien abduction experience and cites the case of

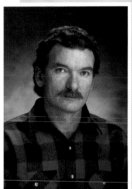

Arizona forestry worker Travis Walton (left).

On November 5, 1975, driving home from work, Walton and six colleagues encountered "a metallic disk hovering in the air, glowing." Walton left the truck to investigate but was allegedly zapped by a "bolt of energy" from the object. His colleagues panicked and drove off, but then turned back to rescue their mate. They were too late—Walton was gone.

Five days later, Walton was found naked and delirious in a phone box. It wasn't until months later that his incredible tale of alien abduction emerged, the full details of which are recounted at length in his bestselling book Fire in the Sky (and the less successful film of the same name).

Could Walton have come face to face with a glowing earthlight? Was the alien ray a spark of energy sparking off it?

On the meteor trail

THE EARTH PASSES THROUGH ABOUT TWENTY CLOUDS OF METEORS EVERY YEAR —SEEN FROM EARTH AS "SHOOTING STARS," SOMETIMES AT A RATE OF ONE EVERY FEW MINUTES. UNSURPRISINGLY, MANY METEOR SHOWERS ARE REPORTED AS UFOS.

In 1772, renowned scientist and "father of modern chemistry" Antoine Laurent Lavoisier was sent by the Academy of Sciences in Paris to investigate a rock that had supposedly fallen out of the sky onto a field. No one in pre-Revolution Paris had any knowledge of such unidentified objects falling to Earth, not even the prestigious scientists.

Lavoisier visited the peasants who had reported the rock and pronounced superciliously: "There are no stones in the sky, therefore no stones can fall from the sky." Subsequent reports of falling stones were denounced as the ignorant mutterings of superstitious peasants. Even a signed petition from an entire village bombarded with rocks in 1790 failed to be taken seriously.

LOSING HIS HEAD

Years later, as our knowledge of the sky became more advanced, these stones were, of course,

METEOR CALENDER

METEOR NAME	DATE	NOTES
QUADRANTIDS	January 1–6	Fast-moving blue trails with yellow fireballs
H-AQUARIDS	April 19–24	Fast moving
LYRIDS	June 10–21	Modest blue streaks, come in short bursts
D-AQUARIDS	July 15 – August 15	Very slow and very long trails
PERSEIDS	July 25 – August 18	Fast and brightly trained; up to 100 meteors an hour
CYGNIDS	August 18–22	Bright white bolides
ORIONIDS	October 16–26	Fast, bright trails
TAURIDS	October 10 – November 30	Slow, bright white fireballs
LEONIDS	November 15–19	Fast; expect a spectacular storm in 1999
GEMINIDS	December 7–15	Brilliant white, no trains; up to 80 meteors an hour

LEFT: *Antoine Lavoisier, the father of modern chemistry, epitomizes the scientific debunker. Like many modern UFO cynics, he would not listen to witnesses of the "unexplained" and refused to believe in meteors, despite evidence literally falling out of the sky.*

shown to be meteorites. Lavoisier, in the meantime, lost his head to the guillotine, and historians mostly chose to overlook this episode of scientific intractability that, for many, epitomizes science's attitude to the unexplained.

GETTING YOUR FACTS STRAIGHT

To rule out meteors from an investigation, you must know what to look for and when. Meteors are generally seen at a height of about 60–75 miles, although many witnesses report seeing them at cloud level. In hilly or built-up areas, witnesses also report seeing a UFO land just behind a hill, building, or growth of trees, when in fact they've seen a meteor up to 80 miles away. Fireballs (see right) lose their intensity well above the ground, and at night will not be seen above 12 miles above ground.

Reports of nocturnal lights and UFOs that leave trails can be correlated with known dates of intense meteor showers. An increase in BOL sightings between July 25 and August 18 for example, when the Earth passes through the Perseids meteor shower, would suggest that the UFO was a meteor.

WHAT ARE YOU LOOKING AT?

• **METEOROIDS** *These are pieces of space debris (usually dead comets), ranging in size from grains of dust to pebbles, that move around the Sun in swarms.*

• **METEORS** *When the Earth passes through meteoroid swarms, we see streaks of light we call shooting stars. These are meteors—space debris that enters Earth's atmosphere at between 5 and 30 miles/second. Because of their speed, they are vaporized by air friction and leave trails of light.*

• **METEORITES** *These are the larger pieces of debris—meteoric rock—that survive the assault from air friction and reach the ground.*

• **BOLIDES** *These are a type of meteor—ones that explode during flight.*

• **FIREBALLS** *These are meteors that appear brighter than any star or planet. Bolides and fireballs can be seen from great distances, often up to 200 miles away, but can appear very close. Pilots sometimes swerve to avoid fireballs that would have been many miles away.*

BELOW: *Meteors are identified by their burning tails of light as they streak through the sky. Ufologists should be aware of the dates on which meteor showers are likely.*

Seeing stars and planets

VENUS, MARS, AND JUPITER WERE ONCE THOUGHT TO BE SOURCES OF ALIEN LIFE, BUT SPACE EXPLORATION HAS NOW PROVED THIS TO BE WRONG. HOWEVER, COULD THE PLANETS STILL BE RESPONSIBLE FOR REPORTS OF UFOS?

On January 7, 1948, residents of Owensboro and Maysville, Kentucky, alerted police to a UFO traveling through the afternoon sky. The police informed the control tower at nearby Godman Air Field, and at 2:45 that afternoon, five National Guard P-51 Mustangs, lead by Captain Thomas Mantell, were dispatched to intercept the object.

RIGHT: *According to some reports, Captain Thomas Mantell's body was never found. Others claim he was refused an open coffin because of his "extraordinary wounds."*

22,000 FEET AND CLIMBING

At 14,000 feet, Mantell radioed the control tower and described the object as "metallic and tremendous in size." By 22,000 feet, all the Mustangs except Mantell had turned back, defeated by lack of oxygen. Mantell had kept climbing, keeping the object in his sights. Then, at about 3:15 P.M., visual contact with Mantell was lost. Two hours later, Mantell's body was found, mangled in his plane wreckage, on a farm near Franklin, Kentucky. His watch had stopped at 3:18, the assumed time of impact with the ground.

CHASING VENUS

The US Air Force issued a report claiming that Mantell had merely been mistakenly chasing the planet Venus. Giving little thought to his oxygen requirements, he then simply blacked out.

Often used to explain UFOs, Venus certainly accounts for quite a few sightings. Given the right conditions, Mercury, Venus, Mars, Jupiter, and Saturn can all be seen from Earth with the naked eye. Venus is the brightest (many WWII pilots mistook it for an enemy plane), but the others, and many of the brighter stars, can also appear as glowing orbs, often on or near the horizon.

RETURNING TO THE SCENE

When investigating a UFO report with the hallmarks of a planet sighting, try to return to

ABOVE: *A planisphere is a useful tool for assessing the position of the stars during any given night. In order to rule out stars as the cause of a UFO report, ufologists can return to the scene of the sighting, line up the planisphere, and determine which stars would have been visible (assuming the weather was clear).*

the scene and scan the horizon for large, bright stars. Do this as soon after the event as possible, since the stars' positions obviously shift. If you're investigating a sighting more than a few weeks later, take a planisphere to the scene. This simple, inexpensive tool, sold at observatories, shows the stars' positions for any time of the year.

CONSIDER OTHER FACTORS

Of course, discovering that a bright star or planet was in the relevant part of the sky does not mean that the case is solved. Other factors, such as cloud cover or the orientation of the witness, may rule out stars as an explanation.

Check with a meteorological office for weather conditions at the time of the alleged UFO sighting, and make sure the witness is absolutely sure of his or her position in relation to the constellations.

SIGHTINGS OF SATURN?

On January 16, 1958, crew members of the Brazilian Navy ship Almirante Saldanha, *anchored off Trinidade Island in the South Atlantic, saw a Saturnlike object (SLO) fly above the island. Civilian Almira Barauna took six photos of the SLO, processed immediately in an ad hoc darkroom before anyone could tamper with them. Later digital analysis proved them to be genuine. In 1994, UFOlogist Steuart Campbell stated that the object was in fact Saturn. A combination of temperature inversion and a mirage of the planet, he claimed, gave the impression that the planet was a mechanical object flying over the island.*

ABOVE: *One of the photographs taken by Almira Barauna of the Saturnlike object over Trinidade Island in January 1958. Could it be Saturn?*

Man-made UFOs

THE SKIES ARE INCREASINGLY CROWDED WITH ALL MANNER OF ORDINARY – AND EXTRAORDINARY – FLYING VEHICLES, MANY OF WHICH ARE REPORTED AS UFOS. INVESTIGATORS MUST BE ABLE TO RECOGNIZE JUST WHAT THESE ARE.

Sightings of aircraft and other man-made flying machines undoubtedly account for a large number of UFO reports, especially when seen at night. The number of UFOs reported along the approach paths to Heathrow Airport, for example, is surprisingly high.

ABOVE: *The impressive panorama of Area 51 at night. For years, this facility did not officially exist or appear on any maps. Many ufologists believe that this was because alien beings were housed there, and many researchers were witness to bizarre aerial phenomena above the base.*

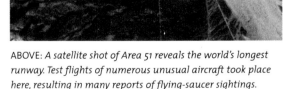

ABOVE: *A satellite shot of Area 51 reveals the world's longest runway. Test flights of numerous unusual aircraft took place here, resulting in many reports of flying-saucer sightings.*

AREA 51

During the early 1990s, a trip to Area 51 – the Nellis Air Force Range and Nuclear Test Site – at Groom Lake, Nevada, would usually guarantee you a "UFO" sighting of some kind. Bright lights, often of differing or varying color, would zip erratically through the sky, performing seemingly impossible maneuvers that would kill any living creature on board. Other objects, silent and motionless, would appear and disappear in and out of the night sky.

ABOVE: *The triangular shape of the impressive F117 Stealth bomber – and the fact that it was test flown over populated areas – suggests that it may have been responsible for the wave of "Black Triangle" UFO reports across Europe.*

KNOW YOUR AIRCRAFT

There are, of course, claims that these vehicles are reverse-engineered alien craft that crashed to Earth and were then recovered by the military. One Robert Lazar, for example, announced in 1989 that he had worked on the reverse-engineering and test-flying of one of nine alien flying saucers at Area 51. However, his claims and credentials as a physicist have been refuted by numerous researchers, and the reality of "Black Project" aircraft such as the F117A Stealth bomber and unmanned aerial vehicles (UAVs) suggests that an extraterrestrial explanation does not need to be found for the bizarre happenings. Similar odd tales could be told from top-secret military facilities the world over. However, a review of the craft known to have been developed suggests that most of what was being seen was test flights of top-secret developmental aircraft.

IN FLIGHT

Ordinary aircraft are often mistaken for UFOs, so researchers should be aware of the standard positions and colors of the major aircraft lights in order to rule out misperceptions.

IN-FLIGHT LIGHTS
Left wing tip: red, continuous

Right wing tip: green, continuous

Leading edge of each wing: white, continuous

Top and bottom of fuselage: red, flashing (about 1 pulse per second)

Over top of each wing: white, continuous

LANDING/RUNWAY LIGHTS
Both wing tips, near leading edge, retractable: white, continuous

Intersection of wing and fuselage: white, taxiing only

Wheel wells: white

(NB: Landing lights are required to be on when aircraft fly below 10,000 feet)

Exotic craft

ALSO OF INTEREST TO THE UFOLOGIST ARE THE TYPES OF EXPERIMENTAL AIRCRAFT THAT ARE, OR HAVE BEEN, REPORTED AS UFOs.

At the turn of the century, in the days before airspace regulation, amateur pilots often built their own airships, leading to speculation that ETs were visiting Earth. The first known UFO vigil took place in 1897, after a "mystery airship" buzzed the town of Everest in Kansas. The same appears to continue today, with keen inventors and the military test-flying experimental aircraft, often without the knowledge of the aviation authorities.

Following is a selection of the types of "exotic" and not widely known man-made craft.

FLYING SAUCERS

The saucer shape is important to aircraft designers. Not only is it able to carry greater payloads than traditional aircraft, the saucer also allows for aerodynamic efficiency, less drag, structural rigidity, radar stealth, and stall resistance. In addition, a saucer could utilize vertical take-off and landing (VTOL), negating the need for long runways. The military has been researching saucers since at least 1942.

AERODYNE Another VTOL flying saucer was the Aerodyne, a 13.5-meter-diameter craft designed and built in the 1950s by the French aircraft designer René Couzinet.

AVROcar See pictured, right.

TARIELKA See pictured, right.

STEALTH CRAFT

Many classified projects were established to research the stealth capabilities of aircraft, and secret tests were carried out without authority from aviation organizations. One of the latest experimental craft possibly being reported as a UFO is known (probably incorrectly) as Aurora, a top-secret Black Budget project originally run out of Area 51.

A-12 ADVANCED TECHNICAL AIRCRAFT (ATA) Another famous Black Project was the McDonnell Douglas A-12 ATA. Nicknamed the "Dorito," after the triangular corn chip, the A-12 was a highly classified stealth triangle that was withdrawn in 1991. Its shape closely resembled UFO descriptions given by witnesses, but it never saw any service other than some test flights.

NORTHROP B-2 SPIRIT STEALTH BOMBER See pictured, right.

UAVs/RPVs

Unmanned aerial vehicles (UAVs) and remotely piloted vehicles (RPVs) are ultralight aerial craft used for reconnaissance and spying or atmospheric research. These, too, are developed under a cloak of secrecy and are often test flown over air-force bases. **DARK STAR** See pictured, right.

RIGHT: **AVROcar** *The Canadian aircraft manufacturer A. V. Roe began work on the V2-9A AVROcar in 1952, with financial backing from the US Air Force. The AVROcar traveled on a cushion of air, but didn't get very far off the ground. The project ended in 1961, when the USAF pulled the funding. Some theorists believe that the project was a cover story to hide the fact that the USAF was actually testing a captured ET vehicle.*

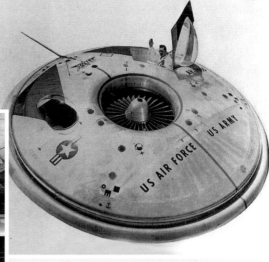

ABOVE: **TARIELKA** *In the early 1980s, Russian space engineer Lev Shukin began work on the Tarielka (Saucer), which was test-flown successfully on a number of occasions. Shukin—who worked on the Mir Space Station project—hopes rather optimistically that it will one day succeed conventional passenger aircraft.*

LEFT: **NORTHROP B-2 SPIRIT STEALTH BOMBER** *The "flying wing" B-2 stealth bomber is not only triangular in shape, but looks strangely disklike when seen from the front. The "black triangle" flap over Europe in 1989–90 was attributed by many to test flights of the B-2 bomber or similar craft.*

RIGHT: **THE TIER III MINUS DARK STAR** *is the latest in UAV technology. Its shape is not typical of that reported by most UFO witnesses, but it, and other remotely piloted craft like it, have nevertheless been implicated in a number of sightings.*

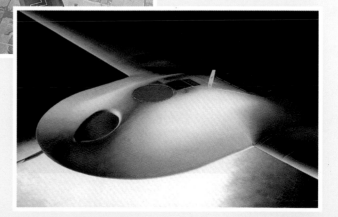

Black helicopters

WHY ARE HELICOPTERS OFTEN REPORTED ALONG WITH STORIES OF CATTLE MUTILATIONS OR UFO SIGHTINGS? ARE THE MILITARY MONITORING ANOMALOUS AERIAL ACTIVITY, OR IS THE EXPLANATION MUCH STRANGER ...?

A common feature of early cattle mutilation cases was "mysterious" helicopters, often reported as being black, unmarked, and silent. According to a 1974 *Newsweek* article entitled "The Midnight Marauder," helicopters were reported over farmland during periods of mutilations, and chasing farm staff at nights. There have been various explanations over the years for this.

DRUG BARONS In the 1970s, the common answer was that the helicopters were ferrying marijuana growers to stands of hemp growing naturally in parts of North America.

RUSTLERS One theory suggested that cattle rustlers were using helicopters, and that they were cutting out organs to use as lures for free-roaming cattle.

OIL COMPANIES Other possible culprits were said to include oil companies, covertly removing organs to assess the mineral content of land.

CULTS Cults practicing ritual blood ceremonies were also accused, based on the discovery of satanic paraphernalia close to a mutilation site.

MILITARY RESEARCH Military/government agencies were researching chemical and biological weaponry, claimed one group of researchers.

The first public suggestion of an otherworldly explanation came from a law enforcement officer. Sheriff Lou Girodo, from Colorado, believed they could be craft "camouflaged as helicopters," and that "it's possible that these mutilations are being done by creatures from outer space."

RIGHT: *Investigators inspect a badly mutilated carcass in an attempt to account for inexplicable wounds.*

ABOVE: *The presence of unmarked helicopters around the time and place of mutilations suggests that there may be a connection.*

ABOVE: *Witnesses Betty Cash and Vicki Landrum reported seeing a UFO escorted by a fleet of Chinook CH-47s. Were the military accompanying a recovered flying saucer?*

DIAMOND OF FIRE

Helicopters played a major part in the story of Betty Cash and Vicki Landrum. On December 29,

1980, while driving to their home town of Dayton, near Houston, the two women witnessed a "diamond of fire" in the sky above the highway. A cloud of about twenty-four black helicopters appeared, encircling and following the object. MUFON researcher John Schussler concluded that the copters were Chinook twin-blades, probably CH-47s. These large, military helicopters are normally used for troop or cargo transport, and often carry heavy, slung loads.

When investigating reports that mention helicopters, remember that all aircraft must file flight plans with air traffic centers. Contact nearby military and civilian air bases and airports for a record of flight activity at the time of the sighting. If this proves fruitless, find a comprehensive book and ask the witness to look through and identify the helicopter. This may give some clues as to its source. If you're investigating helicopter reports as part of a mutilation case, talk informally with locals regarding any known rustlers who might have the means to use helicopters.

FLIGHTS OF FANCY

In his report "UFO Crash Retrievals: Amassing the Evidence," respected UFO researcher Leonard Stringfield details an interview between UFO researcher Tommy Blann and a US Air Force Colonel, referred to as "Colonel X." Colonel X claimed that the US military reserves fleets of unmarked helicopters in isolated or underground bases solely for the purpose of monitoring UFO activity or recovering crashed saucers.

ABOVE: *Leonard Stringfield was the first major ufologist to take reports of crash UFOs seriously.*

Another military insider, known as "Falcon," made a similar revelation regarding the Cash-Landrum affair. "The craft that was observed was an alien craft piloted by military aircraft pilots," Falcon claimed. "They radioed that they thought the craft was going to crash – standard procedures for the military in any situation where an aircraft was going to crash ..." Unfortunately, Falcon went on to reveal that the government was in possession of alien beings, and that their favorite food was strawberry ice cream.

UFO ID ...
the unusual suspects

OVER THE FOLLOWING PAGES IS A GALLERY OF COMMON UFO TYPES, ARRANGED IN
A SOMEWHAT ARBITRARY CLASSIFICATION SYSTEM BASED PRIMARILY ON SHAPE.

The seven divisions of the following guide are: disk, cylinder, spheroid, angular, triangular, balls-of-light (BOLs), and exotic. These are by no means exhaustive, although the last, rather catch-all, category can encompass any number of reports.

The objects chosen to illustrate each division are taken from actual eyewitness reports and represent a typical example of that particular classification of UFO. There is neither the room nor the necessity to present every type of UFO, as the objects reported are as varied as the witnesses reporting them. And rarely is the same object reported twice, unless it is one that can be quickly and easily explained in terms of terrestrial activity.

WITNESS REPORTS

When dealing with UFO witnesses, it is important to establish the shape and characteristics of the object or objects seen. Make sure the witnesses recount their experience in full and draw as detailed a sketch as possible. Then, once this information is logged, show witnesses the following chart and have them identify the shape that corresponds most closely to their sighting. Log the classification number on a UFO

report form for future reference (*see* below). (If the sighting does not conform to any of the following shapes, it should be logged as "exotic.")

Finally, ask witnesses to explain any differences between the selected shape and the actual object encountered. In particular, note any protrusions or surface details.

The purpose of this exercise is to help you establish whether or not the witness is reporting accurately, honestly, consistently, and without embellishment each time. The more the descriptions and drawings differ, the less valuable is the testimony. It should also help you come to some sort of conclusion as to what the object is.

DISK

CATEGORY: *Disk, bi-convex, domed*
WITNESS: *Robert Lazar*
SIGHTED: *Nellis Air Force Range and Nuclear Test Site (Area 51), Nevada, USA*
DATE: *1985*
DIMENSIONS: *40' diameter, 16' height*
NOTES: *In December 1988, Robert "Bob" Lazar claimed to have been employed by the US military to back-engineer one of nine recovered alien craft within Area 51. The Sports Model, so named because of its sleek appearance, was test flown in the Nevada desert. Lazar's claims have yet to be satisfactorily confirmed or refuted.*

CATEGORY: *Disk, conic, domed*
WITNESS: *George Adamski*
SIGHTED: *Desert Center, California, USA*
DATE: *November 20, 1952*
DIMENSIONS: *29' 6" diameter*
NOTES: *Adamski, the world's most famous contactee, was on a saucer hunt with his friends when he witnessed this "beautiful small craft" land in the California desert. After communicating telepathically with its Venusian occupant, Adamski was invited to view the ship in detail. He described the exterior as "translucent and of exquisite color" and surrounded by some form of powerful forcefield.*

CATEGORY: *Disk, bi-convex, lenticular*
WITNESS: *Captain Kenju Terauchi and the crew of Japan Air Lines flight 1628*
SIGHTED: *At 39,000 feet, near Anchorage, Alaska*
DATE: *November 17, 1986*
DIMENSIONS: *unknown ("two times bigger than an aircraft carrier" according to Terauchi)*
NOTES: *This Unidentified Air Traffic (UAT) was not only seen by the Japan Air crew, but tracked on radar by the US Federal Aviation Authority. It remained about 12 miles from JAL 1628 for about 35 minutes, pacing the aircraft. By the time a military Hercules arrived to confirm the sighting, the UAT had gone.*

CYLINDER

CATEGORY: *Cylinder, tubular*
WITNESS: *David Spoor*
SIGHTED: *Norfolk, England*
DATE: *August 19, 1997*
DIMENSIONS: *n/a*
NOTES: *While working in his yard, Spoor spied this self-illuminated craft traveling from east to west across the sky. Around the craft, but seemingly not attached, bright, strobelike lights flashed, and there was no sound. Spoor had enough time to video the object, but analysis has yet to provide an answer. Spoor—and, independently, a local prison officer, Peter Wrigglesworth—continue to film anomalous objects in the sky above Norfolk.*

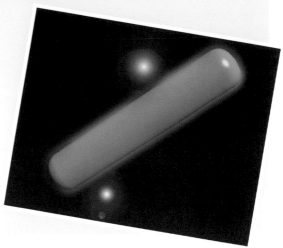

CATEGORY: *Cylinder, tubular*
WITNESS: *Stephen Michalak*
SIGHTED: *Falcon Lake, Manitoba, Canada*
DATE: *May 20, 1967*
DIMENSIONS: *32' x 11' 6"*
NOTES: *Michalak observed two cigar-shaped objects, one of which landed near him. After watching the craft and taking notes, he approached it and touched its golden surface, resulting in the melting of his gloves. As the object departed, a blast of air vented out of a grill in its side, giving Michalak first-degree burns. He also suffered a period of skin infections, nausea, diarrhea, and weight loss, and required examination by 27 doctors.*

CATEGORY: *Cylinder, missile*
WITNESS: *Captain Achille Zaghetti*
SIGHTED: *At 22,000 feet, approaching southeastern coast of England*
DATE: *April 21, 1991*
DIMENSIONS: *10' long*
NOTES: *Zaghetti, captaining an Alitalia McDonald Douglas MD-80, and his co-pilot, radioed Heathrow Airport Air Traffic Control (ATC) with their sighting of a brown-colored missile about 1,000 feet above them. ATC confirmed this sighting when they replied that they had an unidentified object on radar 10 miles behind the MD-80 and traveling at about 350 mph.*

SPHEROID

CATEGORY: *Spheroid, oval*
WITNESS: *Patrolman Sergeant Dionicio "Lonnie" Zamora*
SIGHTED: *Socorro, New Mexico, USA*
DATE: *April 24, 1964*
DIMENSIONS: *n/a*
NOTES: *While pursuing a speeding Chevrolet, Zamora heard what he thought was an exploding dynamite store. He abandoned the pursuit and drove to investigate, only to witness a shiny oval craft "parked" in desert scrub. The object was perfectly smooth, with girderlike legs and a red insignia. Outside were two "people in white coveralls," who retreated inside when Zamora approached. A flame erupted from the underside of the craft as it took off into the sky.*

CATEGORY: *Spheroid, spherical*
WITNESS: *Robert Taylor*
SIGHTED: *Livingstone, Scotland*
DATE: *November 9, 1979*
DIMENSIONS: *20' diameter*
NOTES: *While inspecting a tree farm at Livingstone, forester Taylor encountered a hazy, semitransparent object hovering in a clearing in the trees. Protruding out from a flange along the equator of the object were a series of stationary, bow-tie-shaped propellors; above the flange ran a number of portholes. In addition to this main object, two smaller sea-mine-shaped objects appeared and dragged Taylor away by the trouser legs, and he passed out.*

CATEGORY: *Spheroid, ovoid*
WITNESS: *Maurice Masse*
SIGHTED: *Valensole, France*
DATE: *July 1, 1965*
DIMENSIONS: *8' x 10–11'*
NOTES: *In a case very similar to that of Lonnie Zamora's, Masse, a lavender farmer, heard and then saw a "machine" supported by six legs in his lavender bushes. Outside the object were two bald beings about 3 feet tall wearing green "ski-suits." As Masse approached, one of the beings pointed a small rod at him, immobilizing him for 15 minutes while they boarded the craft through a sliding door and took off into the morning sky.*

ANGULAR

CATEGORY: *Angular, polyhedron*
WITNESS: *Betty Cash, Vicki Landrum, Colby Landrum*
SIGHTED: *Near Huffman, Texas, USA*
DATE: *December 29, 1980*
DIMENSIONS: *n/a*
NOTES: *While driving toward Dayton, Texas, the witnesses saw a "diamond of fire" ahead of them. It drifted out of the sky and hovered above the road, and all three left their car to investigate. Cash, who remained outside the car for the longest period, suffered burns, diarrhea, hair loss, and impaired sight. Before it departed, the diamond became surrounded by Chinook helicopters, which may have been chasing or escorting it.*

CATEGORY: *Angular, star-shaped*
WITNESS: *Multiple, including pilot Frederick Valentich (probably), and Roy Manifold (who photographed it).*
SIGHTED: *Bass Strait, Australia*
DATE: *October 21, 1978*
DIMENSIONS: *n/a*
NOTES: *A UFO flap in Australia reached its peak with this sighting, which infamously resulted in the disappearance of pilot Valentich, who encountered the object at 4,500 feet. His last words, radioed to Melbourne ground control, failed to describe the object that vanished out of the sky and took him and his Cessna with it, but witnesses on the ground described seeing a green, star-shaped object.*

CATEGORY: *Angular, boomerang*
WITNESS: *Multiple witnesses, including Bill Grava, an air-traffic controller on duty at the Sky Harbor International Airport, and a retired policeman (anonymous).*
SIGHTED: *Over Paulden, Wickenburg, Glendale, Phoenix, and Scottsdale in Arizona, USA*
DATE: *Early 1997*
DIMENSIONS: *Nearly a mile long*
NOTES: *This massive object was described as a solid, V-shaped object inlaid with white and red lights, and flying silently at 30 mph. It was seen by hundreds of witnesses, and video recorded by dozens, and subsequent analysis has yet to explain what it was.*

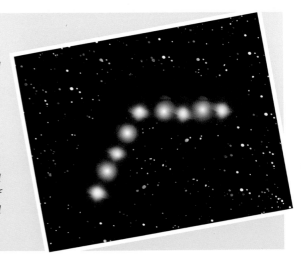

TRIANGULAR

CATEGORY: *Triangular, mantra*
WITNESS: *Frank Kaufmann*
SIGHTED: *Northwest of Roswell, New Mexico, USA*
DATE: *July 7, 1947*
DIMENSIONS: *15' x 23'*
NOTES: *Kaufmann, a member of the US Strategic Air Command, claimed to have been part of a search-and-recover operation initiated after radar evidence indicated the crash of an anomalous "echo." Once at the site, Kaufmann saw this downed ship and the bodies of its crew. The site was quickly secured, and the spacecraft, described as mantra-shaped with a honeycombed underside, was removed to the Roswell Army Air Field.*

CATEGORY: *Triangular, black triangle*
WITNESS: *Professor Leon Brenig*
SIGHTED: *Beaufays Region, Liège, Belgium*
DATE: *March 18, 1990*
DIMENSIONS: *n/a*
NOTES: *Physics professor Brenig was one of more than 2,000 people who witnessed a "Black Triangle" during a wave of sightings that took place in Belgium between 1989 and 1990. The object, which was at an estimated altitude of 500–1,000 feet, was bathed in a yellow glow and had a throbbing red light in the center. According to Brenig, it was completely silent and did not behave like an ordinary aircraft.*

CATEGORY: *Triangular, conic*
WITNESS: *Ron & Paula Watson*
SIGHTED: *Mount Vernon, Missouri, USA*
DATE: *July 1983*
DIMENSIONS: *n/a*
NOTES: *The Watsons first noticed this conic craft when flashes of reflecting sunlight caught their eyes. Using binoculars, they saw what they described as two silver-suited humanoids levitating a dead cow toward the object, which was almost invisible owing to its mirror-like surface reflecting the grass and sky. The cow floated up a ramp into an opening in the cone, closely followed by the aliens, and the craft vanished into thin air.*

BOLS (Balls of light)

CATEGORY: *Balls of light, Earthlights*
WITNESS: *Multiple witnesses*
SIGHTED: *Yakima Indian Reservation, Washington, USA*
DATE: *1970–*
DIMENSIONS: *n/a*
NOTES: *Since the 1970s, wardens and visitors at the reservation have been reporting BOLs dancing along the rocky ridges that cut through the park. This light activity peaks on the run-up to earthquakes in the area and this—combined with other evidence such as reports of glowing clouds—suggest that the BOLs are earthlights. Similar phenomena were also witnessed and researched to a great extent at Hessdalen Valley, Norway.*

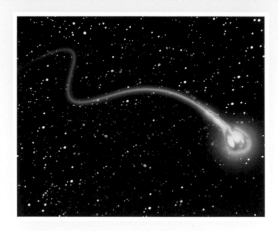

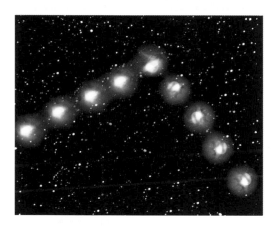

CATEGORY: *Balls of light, string of pearls*
WITNESS: *Multiple witnesses*
SIGHTED: *Lubbock, Texas, USA*
DATE: *August 1951*
DIMENSIONS: *n/a*
NOTES: *This V-shaped formation was often seen traveling over Lubbock at speeds of 375 to 950 mph. Residents of Lubbock—the birthplace of singer Buddy Holly—have reported various numbers of lights and colors. The lights appear on radar, but attempts to intercept them have failed. Explanations include light reflecting off the underbellies of geese or plovers, experimental aircraft, or an unknown meteorological phenomenon.*

CATEGORY: *Balls of light, golden orbs*
WITNESS: *Multiple witnesses*
SIGHTED: *Nevada State Highway 375, Nevada Desert, USA*
DATE: *1990–*
DIMENSIONS: *n/a*
NOTES: *Bright "miniature suns" have been witnessed from this part of Nevada since about 1990. These BOLs hover for a few moments before either fading out or heading for the ground, leaving a vapor trail, and are often seen surrounded by strobing lights. These lights are seen on or around Area 51, so the most probable answer is that they are magnesium flares used in military exercises. The strobing lights may be helicopters monitoring maneuvers.*

EXOTIC

CATEGORY: *Exotic, flying cross*
WITNESS: *RAF Intelligence Officer J. B. W. (Angus) Brooks*
SIGHTED: *Moigne Downs, Dorset, England*
DATE: *October 26, 1967*
DIMENSIONS: *175' span*
NOTES: *While out walking his dog on a windy fall morning, Brooks took shelter in a hollow from the force-8 gale and noticed this silent, translucent craft flying toward him. Initially, one of the "fuselages" pointed in the direction of travel, with the other three together at the rear. Then, as the craft hovered at 200–300 feet, two of the rear fuselages moved outward, forming a perfect cross.*

CATEGORY: *Exotic, pyramid*
WITNESS: *Haroldo Westendorff*
SIGHTED: *5,500 feet above Pelatos, Brazil*
DATE: *October 5, 1996*
DIMENSIONS: *300' wide at base, 150' high*
NOTES: *While flying his Embraer aircraft, Westendorff, an aerobatics pilot, witnessed this rotating pyramid flying silently at an estimated 60–65 mph. A dome on the top of the craft retracted, and a disk-shaped craft emerged and shot off toward the Atlantic. Then, the pyramid's speed of rotation increased, shafts of red light beamed out of the hole in the top, and it shot off at an estimated 7,500 mph. Air traffic controllers confirmed the sighting.*

CATEGORY: *Exotic, rectangular*
WITNESS: *Jan Wolski*
SIGHTED: *Emilcin, Poland*
DATE: *May 10, 1978*
DIMENSIONS: *16' x 8' x 10'*
NOTES: *Farmer Wolski was invited aboard this bizarre craft by two humanoids he had encountered while inspecting his farm. The craft hummed "like bumblebees in flight" and hovered ten feet above the ground. On the corners of the craft were corkscrewlike rods that were rotating rapidly. Wolski entered the craft via a hoist, which was suspended over the entranceway by cables. After a physical examination inside the craft, Wolski was released.*

CHAPTER TWO

Landings

The empiricist thinks he believes only what he sees, but he is much better at believing than at seeing.

GEORGE SANTAYANA

Moving on from strange sights in the sky, what happens when the evidence hits the ground? If ufology has any hope of gaining mainstream acceptance, it is through the serious analysis of physical evidence. Eyewitness testimony may suffice for a court of law, but in the sceptical world of ufology, it counts for very little.

CLOSE ENCOUNTERS

In the Hynek classification system, cases involving evidence of actual interaction between UFOs and the environment are labeled Close Encounters of the Second Kind. They encompass a wide range of evidence: ground traces such as scorch marks and depressions, cellular mutation of plants, physical and physiological damage to animals and humans, electrical interference in equipment and vehicles, and physical remnants such as debris from crashed craft.

Part of your remit as a ufologist is to collect and diligently evaluate physical evidence. Most examples will have a prosaic explanation, and the more carefully your evidence is obtained, the better chance you will have of passing judgment.

MAIN PICTURE: *Crop formation at Alton Barnes, Wiltshire, England. During the 1980s, the crop-circle phenomenon was often presented as concrete, physical proof of alien visitation. To others, crop glyphs were a sign of the gullibility of the "faithful." Whatever the truth, these formations at least offer researchers the chance for hands-on field research.*

RIGHT: *The phenomenon of crop circles is nothing new. This seventeenth-century English news story attributes strange happenings in a Hertfordshire oat field to the workings of the devil. One night, the field appeared to be engulfed in flames, and the following morning the crops were found cut down "... as no Mortal Man was able to do the like." It was not until the latter half of the twentieth century, with the term "UFO nests," that the ET connection was made.*

The Mowing-Devil:
Or, Strange NEWS out of
Hartford-shire.

Being a True Relation of a Farmer, who Bargained
with a Poor Mower, about the Cutting down Three Half
Acres of Oats; upon the Mower's asking too much, the Farmer
mer fwore, That the Devil fhould Mow it, rather than he.
And fo it fell out, that that very Night, the Crop of Oat
fhew'd as if it had been all of a Flame; but next Morning
appear'd fo neatly Mow'd by the Devil, or fome Infernal Spirit,
rit, that no Mortal Man was able to do the like.
Alfo, How the faid Oats ly now in the Field, and the Owner
has not Power to fetch them away.

LEFT: *Footprints, such as those found at the site of an alleged UFO landing in Florida in 1965, offer compelling evidence for Close Encounters of the Second Kind (CEII). Unfortunately, footprints are very easy to fake.*

RIGHT: *New Mexico State police officer Gabe Valdez examines a mutilated carcass in Rio Arriba county. The mutilation phenomenon is a subject on the fringe of ufology that offers ufologists yet more tangible evidence for empirical analysis.*

Tracing physical evidence

THE EVIDENCE OF ALIEN CRAFT LANDING ON EARTH IS KNOWN AS PHYSICAL
TRACE EVIDENCE. WHAT EXACTLY SHOULD YOU BE LOOKING FOR?

On November 2, 1971, sixteen-year-old Ronnie Johnson and his parents encountered a mushroom-shaped craft hovering silently over their farm in Delphos, Kansas. Ronnie reported a classic experience: being almost paralyzed and temporarily blinded by the craft. But this was a case with a difference because there remained at the site physical evidence of the craft's presence.

A spectacular ring of phosphorescent dust was left. On touching this, Johnson's mother's fingers became paralyzed and remained numb for several weeks. According to the Johnsons and the principal investigator of the case, Ted Phillips, the soil stayed aglow for four days.

ABOVE: *A photograph of the phosphorescent ring of powder that was famously encountered by the Johnsons in Kansas during the early 1970s. Affected soil was removed for analysis by the main investigator, Ted Phillips.*

EXTRAORDINARY FINDINGS

Phillips, a civil engineer from Missouri who claims to have investigated over 600 such "landing" cases, examined the soil, which was dehydrated to a depth of 5½ inches. He collected two samples—one affected by the craft; the other, unaffected and taken from another part of the farm—and immersed them in water. The control sample dissolved, but the affected soil remained dry. Months later, after a heavy snowfall, Phillips returned to the farm to find the ring of soil still unable to absorb moisture. The credibility of the Johnsons as witnesses has been called into question, but the case does provide tangible physical evidence that can be analyzed.

COLLECTING DATA

When investigating a case involving physical evidence, collect as much data as possible. Take photographs from numerous angles, and include a scale such as the ruler edge of an orienteering compass. Measure distances, depths, widths, and angles, making copious notes and bagging samples in ziplock bags, precisely labeled. Collect more than you need, and collect control samples —specimens such as soil and plants that have not been affected by the suspected alien presence.

BURDEN OF PROOF

Hard physical evidence generally only "counts" when an alien presence has made a physical change to the environment, as described below. Other examples include physiological effects on humans and animals, and cytological mutations in plants.

ABOVE: *The landing gear of the UFO witnessed by police officer Lonnie Zamora left these impressions (sketched left) in the desert soil.*

FOOTPRINTS:
-IN SOFT SAND

Note: 1 SET OF
PRINTS IN AREA
OF # 4 INDENTATION
NOTED - POSSIBLY MORE
Outline Destroyed By Personnel
IN AREA.

x—Depth 2"

12 ½"
IV
Depth ½"
Possible END OF PRINT-
Undetermined Due To Type of Soil

to extract large samples using a tube called a core borer or by cutting out a square with a spade.

FOOTPRINTS *Reports of these are rare, but treat them as you would the landing impressions. Take particular note of the design of the print.*

ABOVE: *UFOs have been known to leave behind oily and slag-like deposits. Such evidence should be collected and analyzed.*

IMPRESSIONS MADE BY LANDING GEAR *Document comprehensively and draw an accurate scale diagram. Note the surrounding conditions (wet, dry, soft, hard) and the impressions (compacted or scooped). If possible, make plaster casts.*

SCORCH MARKS AND BURNS *Look for evidence of the use of a retrobooster for landing or a rocket for take-off. Expect to find scorched earth or chemical deposits. Collect samples for chemical analysis.*

DESSICATED (DRY) SOIL *Measure and document any patches of dessicated ground, and attempt to determine the depth of dessication. You may need*

ALIEN ARTIFACTS *Out-of-place artifacts (OOPARTs) include chemical deposits or metal fragments.*

ENVIRONMENTAL DAMAGE *Check for emergency-landing damage to surrounding trees, buildings, or structures such as electricity pylons.*

LEFT: *After a visit to the Florida home of witness John Reeves in 1966, aliens left behind these footprints. Evidence such as this should be photographed extensively, and plaster casts made in order to give an indication of the size of who or whatever made them.*

Analyzing trace evidence

ASSUMING THAT YOU FIND SOME TRACE EVIDENCE, YOUR NEXT TASK IS TO IDENTIFY WHAT YOU'VE COLLECTED—IN ORDER TO DISTINGUISH THE POTENTIALLY ALIEN FROM THE MUNDANE.

WITNESS TESTIMONY

Begin your analysis of physical evidence by interviewing any witnesses. Ask them:

▶ To what extent did the UFO make contact with the ground or affected area?

▶ Did it touch the surface, or simply come close?

▶ How long did it remain over the affected area?

▶ Did the witness see the UFO interacting with the environment, or just notice the aftereffects?

▶ How much time passed between seeing the UFO and noticing any trace evidence?

▶ Did the UFO affect any other areas or objects—such as trees or buildings—on its approach or departure?

▶ Can its flight path be traced by damage to the environment?

▶ Did the UFO emit any form of visible radiation, or affect the environment with any form of light or laser beam?

▶ Having drawn a map of the area, ask the witness to identify their position and any movements in relation to the affected areas and the flight path of the UFO. Make sure you keep your own series of detailed notes and sketches.

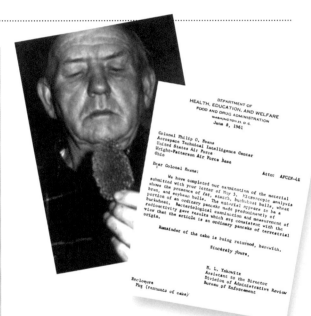

ABOVE: On April 18, 1961, Wisconsin chicken-farmer Joe Simonton witnessed a UFO land in his yard. Three humanoids "resembling Italians" appeared from a hatch and proceeded to cook pancakes before lifting off again. Chemical analysis of the pancakes (report inset) revealed them to be made from nothing very alien: wheat bran, starch, and soybean hulls.

The analysis of an area affected by a UFO—and any collected trace evidence—should be carried out by a trained geologist, agriculturalist, or chemist—or preferably by all three. Analysis by an engineer is also very useful. Knowing that it requires 2,000 pounds to make a 2½-inch depression in grassland, for example, makes it possible to draw conclusions about an object's shape and weight.

TYPES OF ANALYSIS

• CHEMICAL ANALYSIS •

Spectral Analysis: *A spectroscope is used to measure the abundance of elements in the samples. Suitable for artifacts and soil or crop samples collected in ziplock bags or a sealable core-borer.*

Chromatography: *Samples in solution are separated chemically to identify components. Samples must have been collected in a non-plastic container.*

• CELLULAR ANALYSIS •

Microscopy: *Samples are examined with an electron microscope. The size of plant cell pits, through which chemicals flow, can be measured. Crop and plant samples should be collected in ziplock bags.*

• THERMAL ANALYSIS •

Differential analysis: *The samples are heated, and the difference in the change of temperatures and weights are measured.*

Thermoluminescence: *The light emitted as a sample is heated produces a characteristic thermo-luminescence curve. Radiation affects this curve.*

Microwave exposure: *The reaction of the samples to microwave radiation can be analyzed and compared using microscopy. Suitable for soil samples and artifacts collected in ziplock bags.*

• MAGNETIC ANALYSIS •

Magnetrometry: *The magnetic quantities of samples are measured. A basic mapping of the magnetic field can also be made using a compass. Control readings should be made around the affected areas, since magnetometers can register natural fluctuations. Analysis is performed at the site and in the laboratory. The integrity of collected samples must be maintained, as the magnetic field is determined by the individual soil particles. This is done by collection with a sealable core-borer.*

• ELECTRICAL ANALYSIS •

Conductivity: *The conducting power of the samples is measured, identifying the strength of the magnetic field.*

• HYDROLYTIC ANALYSIS •

Permeability: *Samples are immersed in water to assess their ability to diffuse.*

Moisture measurement: *The water content of samples is calculated using a water meter. Suited to soil samples collected in ziplock bags.*

• BIOLOGICAL ANALYSIS •

Embryogenetics: *Seeds can be planted in both affected and control samples, in order to monitor differences in the speed of plant germination. Substantial soil samples are needed.*

• RADIOLOGICAL ANALYSIS •

Radiation monitoring: *A calibrated Geiger counter detects and measures ionizing particles, providing radiation data. Performed at the site and in the laboratory.*

ABOVE: *These fragments of metal—supposedly debris from a crashed flying saucer—were analyzed by American researcher Linda Moulton Howe. The findings were inconclusive.*

Crop circles ... signs from above?

CROP CIRCLES ARE ONE OF THE MOST EXTRAORDINARY AND CONTROVERSIAL OF TRACE PHENOMENA. ARE ALIENS LANDING IN OUR CROPS OR SENDING MESSAGES? OR IS A GROUP OF JOKERS SIMPLY TESTING OUR GULLIBILITY?

In late July 1998, an 89-foot-wide circular pictogram appeared in a field at Huise, near Oudenaarde in Belgium. The symmetrical glyph, flattened out of the long stalks of summer corn, was geometrically precise, with each line of the formation exactly 6½ feet wide. Local ufologists christened the crop circle "The Star of David," due to a six-pointed star emblem in the center. It was one of at least eight such crop formations discovered in Belgium since June.

The crop circle is a relative newcomer to the world of the unknown—a phenomenon of the 1980s that revitalized a tiring UFO industry. Unlike the out-of-focus images that often illustrate ufology, crop circles provided a strong visual focus, and the media leaped at the chance to promote them, irrespective of any evidence of ET intervention. Before long, however, the media grew tired, and by the mid-1990s, the crop circles seemed as dead as flattened corn.

BELOW:*This 151-circle glyph, found next to Stonehenge in July 1996, supposedly materialized within 45 minutes.*

LEFT *(inset): "Cerealogist" Pat Delgado produced this diagram showing the precise mathematical structure of the glyph.*

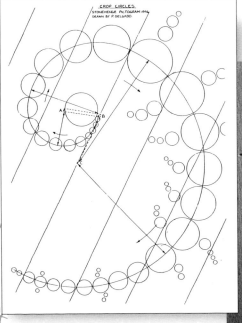

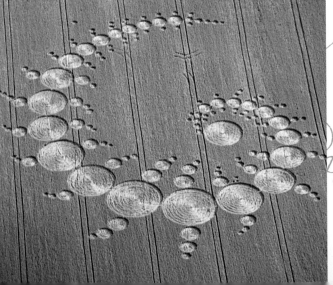

Yet crop circles have not gone away. Each year, accounts of increasingly complex creations are logged. The question is: who creates them?

The answer is most probably humans. The aforementioned "Star of David" was actually "commissioned" from experienced crop-hoaxers by Belgian television. With the benefit of hindsight, researchers spotted the telltale signs of a "man-made" circle; walking in its center didn't feel like walking in the middle of a "real" circle, they said.

Throughout the 1980s, a number of human circle-makers took the credit for producing a significant amount of grain patterns. Some human

ABOVE: *Circle-makers Doug and Dave plan a crop glyph. Often accused of being members of intelligence agencies, human circle-makers have battled with ufologists to prove that they, and not aliens, are responsible for certain circles.*

circle-creaters claim that the original circles began as giant works of art intended to be photographed.

Another theory is that some circles are created by freak meteorological events. Reports of strange lights in fields suggest that a phenomenon similar to earthlights could be responsible. One scientist proposed that plasma vortices—whirlwinds of ionized air—could discharge in or above crops, leveling the stalks evenly. The debate continues ....

THE STORY OF CROP CIRCLES

The extraterrestrial aspect of the crop circle phenomenon began, arguably, in August 1980, when ufologists picked up on a newspaper report of the discovery of a 60-foot-wide circle of flattened oats in Wiltshire, England. Theories emerged that saucers were landing in the English countryside, particularly in fields close to sites of historic importance. Since then, hundreds of similar crop formations have been reported each year throughout the world.

However, the story of the crop circle can be traced back at least 400 years, to a report of a circle that appeared in Assen, Holland, in 1590. Then, as today, theories ranged from the meteorological to the supernatural. The devil himself was often the accused. An account from seventeenth-century England, for example, entitled "The Mowing Devil: Or, Strange NEWS out of Hartford-shire," reported how, on one occasion, three acres of oats were found "so neatly Mow'd by the Devil, or some Infernal Spirit, that no Mortal Man was able to do the like."

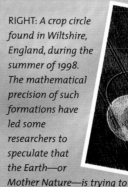

RIGHT: *A crop circle found in Wiltshire, England, during the summer of 1998. The mathematical precision of such formations have led some researchers to speculate that the Earth—or Mother Nature—is trying to communicate some kind of warning to us.*

Unnatural deaths

THE INEXPLICABLE MUTILATION OF CATTLE AND OTHER ANIMALS IS A GENUINE PHENOMENON, ALL TOO VIVIDLY ILLUSTRATED WITH PHOTOS AND PATHOLOGICAL EVIDENCE. BUT DOES ANY OF THIS SUGGEST EXTRATERRESTRIAL CONNECTIONS?

Drained of blood, stripped of flesh from the neck up, and with the spine and internal organs missing—that's how one farmer, Berle Lewis, found an unfortunate colt in his field in Alamosa County, Colorado, in September 1967.

When the colt was autopsied, the areas around the lesions in the hide were found to be very dark, "as if the flesh had been opened and cauterized with a surgical cauterizing blade." Years later, researchers identified these as surgical laser cuts—

technology that was not widespread until the mid-1970s. Also inexplicable was the fact that there were no tracks—animal, human, vehicular, or otherwise—surrounding the carcass.

The most interesting aspect, as far as ufologists are concerned, was a series of holes in a circular arrangement close to the corpse—"a three-foot circle of six or eight holes in the ground about four inches across and three to four inches deep," according to Lewis. What's more, his 87-year-old

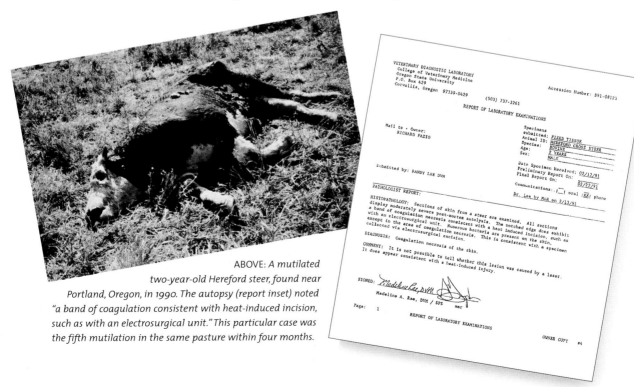

ABOVE: *A mutilated two-year-old Hereford steer, found near Portland, Oregon, in 1990. The autopsy (report inset) noted "a band of coagulation consistent with heat-induced incision, such as with an electrosurgical unit." This particular case was the fifth mutilation in the same pasture within four months.*

mother-in-law claimed to have seen a "large object" pass over the family's ranch the night before. Were ET visitors carrying out gruesome experiments?

A STRANGE HARVEST

Spearheading research into the mutilation phenomenon is Linda Moulton Howe, the American film-maker responsible for the cutting-edge documentary *A Strange Harvest* (1980). Howe first believed the government was behind the mutilations—perhaps to monitor accidental spread of a contaminant—but now thinks aliens are involved.

Of course, cows die in ordinary circumstances all the time. It's ufologists that turn a few bizarre deaths into a "wave." However, there remains a hard core of cases where no explanations can be found.

While it might be in bad taste to look for an over-obvious answer to these mutilations, doing so suggests that humans are the prime suspects. However, the only solid evidence found to support the human connection was a blue satchel (possibly government issue), found on a ranch in Colorado, that contained surgical gloves, a bloody scalpel, and a cow's ear. Unfortunately, no fingerprints could be taken, and the FBI never found the earless cow.

ABOVE: *This image, supposedly showing the Chupacabras, was posted anonymously on the Internet. While probably faked, it does match artists' impressions (right).*

THE GOAT-SUCKER

The animal mutilation phenomenon took on a new twist in early 1995 with an outbreak of bizarre livestock and pet deaths on the Caribbean island of Puerto Rico. At first, dismembered sheep were found—often days after their death, but apparently showing no signs of rigor mortis—with all the hallmarks of a "traditional" mutilation: bloodless, laser-accurate incisions and a lack of tracks. Later, the attacker became less discriminating, butchering rabbits, horses, dogs, cats, birds—even rats.

It is said that the culprit is the feared Chupacabras (goat-sucker)—a 6-foot tall, dark, winged creature with orange eyes and large, sharp claws. Leading the hunt for the Chupacabras is Jorge Martin, editor of the local UFO magazine. He has correlated mutilation cases with UFO sightings, and believes that the Chupacabras is not of this Earth. He has even postulated that the beast could be an alien pet left behind after a trip to Earth. Other suspects are more down-to-earth, including mutated creatures from genetic experiments.

Whatever it is, or wherever it comes from, something is killing Puerto Rican (and now Mexican) livestock, and farmers are fearing for their livelihoods. Just as well, then, that some Puerto Ricans have made a small fortune from their newly realized Chupacabras merchandising.

Mutilations manifest

THE KEY TO ESTABLISHING WHETHER EVIDENCE FROM ANIMAL MUTILATIONS POINTS TO THE EXTRATERRESTRIAL HYPOTHESIS IS THE PROFESSIONAL, METICULOUS COLLECTION OF DATA.

There have been few official investigations into animal mutilation. Assuming bizarre cases to be the work of Satanists, the US Bureau of Alcohol, Tobacco, and Firearms (ATF) started an inquiry in 1975 that turned into an FBI-backed study. The findings – unsurprisingly – stated that no sufficient data had been found to support UFO or strange "conspiracy" theories, but it seems that this investigation left a lot to be desired. The case might be closed as far as governments are concerned, but there are still enough unanswered questions to warrant a serious investigation.

RIGHT: An initiate bites the head off a chicken during a voodoo ceremony. Could the animal mutilations phenomenon be the result of Western cultists performing their own bizarre ceremonies?

ANIMAL HIT LIST

Cows are not the only animals to be found mysteriously mutilated, according to ufologists. Dogs, cats, sheep, ducks, goats, chickens, and deer were found mutilated on Long Island, New York, in January 1988. In some cases, the lower jaws were missing or stripped of flesh; in others, internal organs had been removed; in others still, the heads, legs, eyes, ears, and tongues had been surgically removed.

Shepherds near Santa Rosa in Bolivia witnessed a disk-shaped craft descend on their flock and strike each sheep dead with a bolt of light. On inspection, the sheep were found to be bloodless, with desiccated organs. Even marine life is at risk. This whale (above), found on an English beach after a spate of UFO sightings in the area, had all the hallmarks of a classic mutilation, including exsanguination and missing organs.

FOLLOW THESE STEPS...INVESTIGATING MUTILATIONS

The investigation of mutilated animals will rely on the researcher having access to a willing veterinary pathologist, who should probably not be made aware of the ufological interest in the case. Also, there are a number of steps a ufologist should take to log case notes adequately:

▶ *Quiz the owner of the animal to establish when the victim was last seen alive. Did they see anything unusual in the sky? Have any other animals died in strange circumstances? Neighbors' animals?*

▶ *Photograph the carcass from all angles. Shoot the surrounding area, and tracks that lead to or from the body. Get as close as your nose and stomach will allow, and photograph the wounds in detail.*

▶ *If the owner hasn't called a vet, do so. Have the vet establish the time and cause of death. If possible, ask for a full autopsy, to look out for strange material in the body, particularly the ribcage (putty-like substances have been found in some cases).*

▶ *Look for (or make sure the pathologist looks for) bruises or broken bones. This could suggest that the animal had fallen from a height.*

▶ *Take blood samples and have them analyzed for all-too-earthly tranquilizers such as Atropine.*

▶ *Collect samples of hide that have been lacerated and samples that haven't as controls. Both sets should be sent to a vet for analysis. If possible, keep the samples in a 10 percent formaldehyde solution (or check with the laboratory that will analyze the samples how they would like them stored).*

▶ *Make sure the pathologist establishes how the lacerations were made. If they report anything out of the ordinary, and if finances allow, ask for a set of microscope photographs (photomicrographs).*

▶ *Have evidence assessed by two independent sources. Also, make sure the tests are "double-blind" – that is, the testers are unaware of the circumstances of the case.*

▶ *Check the local press for stories of UFO sightings around the time of the mutilation.*

▶ *A reported feature of some mutilation cases is a marked increase in radiation around the carcass. If possible, have the radioactivity of the area measured and get the figure you obtain assessed by an independent expert.*

▶ *Scan the area surrounding the carcass for possible trace evidence of landed craft. It is important with mutilation cases that you act as quickly as possible. Therefore, it is useful to establish who will assist you in your investigation – vets, laboratories, etc. – in advance.*

In January 1998, the US Air Force announced the development of the Laser Medical Pen, or MedPen. This surgical tool provides battlefield medics with a portable laser scalpel that coagulates blood as it cuts, giving a clean, bloodless incision. Could field tests of this implement account for some cases of mutilation?

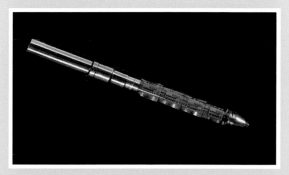

Human traces

WE'VE DISCUSSED POSSIBLE ALIEN TRACES BEING LEFT BEHIND ON THE GROUND ITSELF, OR ON ALL KINDS OF ANIMALS, BUT WHAT ABOUT POSSIBLE EVIDENCE LEFT BEHIND IN HUMANS?

Encounters with UFOs can certainly lead to a confused mental state brought about by fear, but what about any actual physical effects? And what might these tell us about their origins?

Jenny Randles, the leading investigator of the unexplained, coined the phrase "The Oz Factor" to describe an oft-reported altered state of consciousness (ASC) that accompanies an alien encounter experience. In the same way that visions of the Messiah or the Blessed Virgin Mary can bring about a change in mental condition, so too can UFO encounters. In some cases, this can lead to a feeling akin to religious euphoria—or uforia, I suppose. In extreme cases—or exteme witnesses—it can lead to mental stress and even suicide.

ALL IN THE MIND ...

As interesting as these effects are, they are difficult to quantify. In recent years, especially in Europe, ufologists have focused on ASC to explain the whole UFO experience. Taking their lead from psychologist Carl Jung, many researchers believe that aliens come from within the mind, not the universe beyond. As such, alien visitors, in the form of demons, fairies, and so on, have always been with us.

Across the Atlantic, the ET hypothesis remains the more favored explanation for UFO sightings. As a result, there is more acceptance of the physical side-effects of the encounter experience:

PARALYSIS Whether caused by the witness's fear of being abducted or by a genuine alien power, paralysis is a much-reported feature of UFO sightings. The mind does strange things in strange situations, especially given our expectations of alien encounters; however, there have been many notable occasions on which witnesses report being zapped by a paralyzing beam from the UFO.

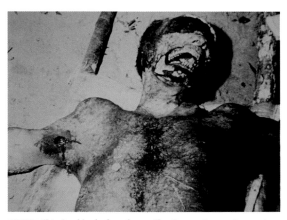

ABOVE: *This dead body, found near the Guarapiranga Reservoir, Brazil, in 1988, displayed many hallmarks of an alien mutilation: flesh was stripped from its jaw; internal organs and genitals had been removed; and the rectum cored out. Were aliens responsible?*

THE BURNING QUESTION

Twenty-three-year-old clerk Denise Bishop was struck on the hand by a "lime-green pencil beam of light" from a UFO in September 1981. The object hovered above the rooftops of Weston Mill, Plymouth, England, and projected shafts of light onto the ground. The beam that hit Bishop immobilized her for 30 seconds. Once indoors, she noticed blood seeping from her hand and realized she had been burned. A surgeon who investigated the wound and the scar that eventually formed concluded that it had all the features of a laser burn.

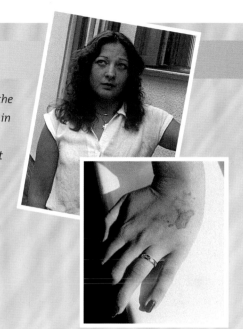

RIGHT: Clerk Denise Bishop reported being zapped by a large, silent, metallic gray UFO as it passed over her home. She claimed to have been paralyzed by the beam of light, and the affected skin (inset) appeared to slough off, revealing fresh skin beneath.

UNCONSCIOUSNESS Less easy to explain in terms of the Oz Factor or uforia are cases in which witnesses are knocked unconscious—in most cases, by some form of beam "weapon" or overpowering light. One of the most famous examples of this involves the case of Travis Walton, who was struck by a ray of light from a UFO in front of his colleagues (*see page 25*).

BURNS A more disturbing example of the physical effects of UFOs dates back to 1946. South American farmer João Prestes Filho was caught in the glow of a blinding light outside his home. After being knocked to the ground by the light, he scrambled up and raced into town for help. He was met by the local fiscal inspector, who witnessed the most horrifying of sights: Filho's flesh began to "cook" and fall away from the bone. Large chunks dropped from every part of his body, leaving an almost skeletal frame. He died on the way to the hospital, and doctors pronounced death from "generalized burns."

RADIATION SICKNESS AND CANCERS Another CEII involving burns is the Cash-Landrum affair of 1980 (*see pages 35 and 40*). The effects were less intense but more long-term, and the survival of witnesses gave investigators a chance to assess the effects. After seeing a UFO in Texas, the witnesses suffered hair loss, eye complaints, vomiting, diarrhea, blistering skin, and, for Betty Cash (who died on the anniversary of the event in 1998), breast cancer that required a mastectomy. The symptoms, which suggest radiation sickness, could not be explained by the many doctors who investigated the trio. Except for unsubstantiated theories that the object was some kind of man-made craft for transporting nuclear waste, the case remains unsolved.

CHAPTER THREE

Encounters

There is no other universe except the human universe, the universe of human subjectivity.

JEAN-PAUL SARTRE

Toward the end of the 1800s, the UFO phenomenon took on a new dimension with the extraterrestrial hypothesis. Spurred on by fledgling science-fiction writers such as Jules Verne and H. G. Wells, and the scientific advancements of the Industrial Revolution, especially in transportation, Victorian skywatchers began to theorize that the lights in the sky seen throughout history were craft from other worlds—a notion still more or less in place today.

THE DAWN OF SAUCEROLOGY

Throughout the early twentieth century, reports dribbled in that today could be classed as Close Encounters of the Third or Fourth kind. However, it wasn't until the 1950s, when a Polish bootlegger named George Adamski announced that he had made contact with "space people" that the era of saucerology began. By the 1960s, claims were pouring in regarding alien-human contact and kidnappings. In 1991, a survey revealed that one in fifty Americans are "probably" abductees. This would mean, worldwide, over 4,500 abductions a day for the past seventy years. The UFO community is divided. Some believe that abductions take place in order to breed half-human, half-alien babies; others renounce the whole area as an elaborate red herring, pumped up by naive ufologists.

MAIN PICTURE: *The "gray" has dominated ufology for over 40 years and has become a modern archetype to rival fairies and demons. Does this mean that it does not exist, or is the consistency of reports proof that alien encounters are universal?*

RIGHT AND BELOW: *New Mexico contactee Paul Villa fired off dozens of photographs of extraterrestrial flying saucers during his alleged meetings with aliens from Coma Berenices. Villa believed that aliens were "a small part of God's huge armies" and that they would "redeem humanity from their present immoral fallen condition"— a message commonly received by alien contactees.*

The extraterrestrial hypothesis states that some UFOs are intelligently controlled extraterrestrial vehicles; the sheer weight of eyewitness testimony to the ETH means that, despite their own beliefs, ufologists must be open to this theory. Only with this balanced approach will any headway be made in the investigation of UFOs.

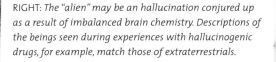

RIGHT: *The "alien" may be an hallucination conjured up as a result of imbalanced brain chemistry. Descriptions of the beings seen during experiences with hallucinogenic drugs, for example, match those of extraterrestrials.*

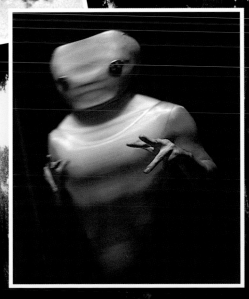

Meeting with the aliens ... the Adamski story

MANY ASPECTS OF UFOLOGY COME AND GO IN WAVES. THE 1950S WERE THE GOLDEN AGE OF FLYING SAUCERY AND ALIEN-HUMAN CONTACT—MUCH OF IT SPARKED BY ONE EXTRAORDINARY MAN.

Although dozens of reports of face-to-face contact between Earthlings and space aliens have since emerged, the so-called "contactee" phenomenon truly began on Thursday, November 20, 1952, when George Adamski, self-proclaimed "philosopher, student, teacher, saucer researcher," met with Orthon, a visitor from Venus.

It was a typically scorching day in the California desert when Adamski ventured out into the noonday sun with six friends. Their intention was "establishing a contact." Adamski had been "tipped off" that the saucers were landing in this part of California, and made regular but unsuccessful trips to photograph them. Today, however, would be different.

After picnicking and taking photos of the stunning scenery, they witnessed a "gigantic cigar-shaped silvery craft, without wings or appendages of any kind" sailing silently through the sky. Adamski separated from the group. He put about half a mile between himself and his companions, but remained in view of them, and came face-to-face with a man with long blond hair, wearing trousers resembling ski-pants and size nine ox-blood red shoes. After a moment, Adamski "realized that I was in the presence of a man from space—A HUMAN BEING FROM ANOTHER WORLD! [his emphasis]." In a form of intergalactic greeting, they touched palms.

The two men communicated through "feelings, signs, and above all, by means of telepathy." Adamski learned that this being came in peace from Venus, and that he and fellow Venusians were anxious about the level of "radiations going out from Earth." Environmental concern, which would become a common feature of many contacts and abductions, was related to the use of nuclear weapons, a fear that gripped 1950s' Cold War America. After more intergalactic chat, Adamski was shown the Venusian's Scout Craft and watched as his new friend climbed on board and took off into the sky.

LEFT: *George Adamski turned the UFO world on its head with his reports of contact with aliens, and heralded a new, almost cultish era of ufology.*

THE SAUCER HAS LANDED

From then on, Adamski took many photographs of flying saucers and cigars. He featured heavily in Desmond Leslie's *Flying Saucers Have Landed* (1953) and became something of a cult figure. In follow-up books, he satisfied his followers' insatiable appetite for stories by going on to claim that he traveled throughout the solar system with his space brothers.

To the modern ufologist, it is difficult to appreciate the effect Adamski and his stories had on the world. To an impressionable, paranoid 1950s audience, his claims encapsulated their fears and hopes; how could we ignore warnings of nuclear armageddon coming from space aliens? But, despite his good intentions and relevant messages, we now know that Adamski was slightly economical with the truth. He was often keen to promote his ties with the Palomar Observatory, although his chief connection was the few

RIGHT: *George Adamski's account of his meeting with Venusians was first published in 1953.*

acquaintances he may have had there and his private property at the base of the mountain. He was also rather vague about his qualifications, and his fantastical stories have since proved to be without foundation following NASA's probing of other planets. And yet he succeeded in shooting dozens of photos and filming some incredible footage that still remains unexplained.

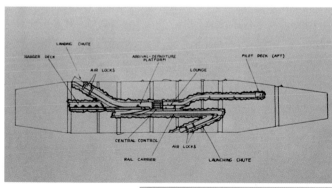

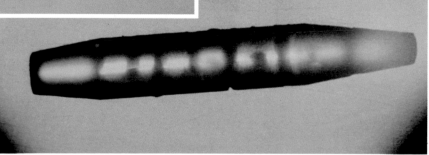

ABOVE: *A drawing of the Venusian mothership by Glenn Passmore from details supplied by George Adamski.* RIGHT: *Cigar-shaped Venusian interplanetary carrier photographed through a 6" telescope over Paloma, California, May 1952.*

Adamski's legacy

IN THE WAKE OF ADAMSKI'S BOLD PRONOUNCEMENTS, OTHER EQUALLY
AUDACIOUS CLAIMS SOON SURFACED.

The 1950s saw a wealth of flying saucers. From this time on, all kinds of amazing "contactee" characters emerged:

ABOVE: *Contactee Daniel Fry (inset) photographed this classic saucer to prove the reality of his encounters with the alien A-lan. The picture, like his claims, has not stood the test of time.*

DANIEL FRY American "Dr." Daniel Fry claimed in 1954 to have been invited aboard a UFO in the White Sands desert on Independence Day 1949. Throughout the 1950s, Fry continued to witness saucers and communicate with their controllers who, like Adamski's, preached eco-warnings.

Fry was told by his contact A-Lan that a former "Earthian" super-race had fled to Mars thousands of years ago and were now re-establishing contact with Earth "for the welfare and preservation" of the planet. Fry was tasked to spread the word, which he duly did in *The White Sands Incident* (1954).

Fry was not the man he made himself out to be. His doctorate came from a nonexistent college, and few of his photographs have stood the test of time or computer analysis.

HOWARD MENGER Another controversial contactee was Howard Menger from New Jersey. Since the age of ten, Menger had supposedly been in contact with space aliens, who suggested that he was a reincarnated Saturnian. In his book *From Outer Space to You* (1959), Menger claims that he acted as a barber for the spacemen and issued underwear

ABOVE: *Howard Menger (seen left with his wife) reported and photographed encounters with UFOs from Venus, Mars, and Saturn.*

to the females. He also discourses at length on alien food. (He once brought back a potato from the Moon and handed it over to the CIA for analysis.) An undisputed fantasist, Menger backed up his incredible claims with photographs. He has largely stuck by his stories to this day and has never profited by his claims.

PAUL VILLA One important contactee who shunned publicity and saw little financial reward was Paul Villa, a US Air Force mechanic who claimed to have made contact with aliens from the Coma Berenices constellation. According to Villa, the aliens taught that "when the law of love rules the minds of men of Earth, then the people of other worlds will come in great numbers."

Again, Villa snapped many photographs, and analysts still debate their authenticity. It has even been suggested that Villa did experience genuine encounters, but built and photographed models in order to convince others.

BILLY MEIER During the 1960s, interesting contactee cases dwindled. The subject had become popularized, and space probes revealed the inhospitable truth about some of the planets that supposedly housed aliens. However, in 1975, Swiss farmer Billy Meier revitalized the phenomenon by communicating with aliens from the Pleiades.

Asket, Plaja, Ptaah, Quetzal, and Semjase met with Billy between 1975 and 1978. Their encounters received enormous publicity, and the photographs were considered some of the best ever. Again, the message was: make love not war, and prevent society's rushing into its own destruction. Researcher Gary Kinder publicized Meier's story in *Light Years* (1987), but astronomical data has effectively ruled out the Pleiades as a source of intelligent life.

INTO THE MILLENNIUM

Contactees continue to emerge. In late 1997, English UFO investigator David Dane showed me over 20 hours' worth of video footage (left) involving two possible contactees from southeastern England. The videos show the two men—David Spoor and Peter Wrigglesworth— apparently communicating with strange, nocturnal lights. Communication between the parties continues to this day, by means of a simple on-off flash code. The footage is the most compelling I've ever seen, and the witnesses are convincing and genuine. If this case turns out to be a classic contactee experience, it will be one of the least sensational but most compelling ever.

ABOVE: *This UFO, shot by contactee Paul Villa at Peralta, New Mexico, supposedly contained nine aliens from Coma Berenices. Villa claimed that the aliens spoke to him for ninety minutes.*

Abduction ...
a walk on the dark side

THE NOW-CLASSIC ABDUCTION TALE OF NEW HAMPSHIRE COUPLE BETTY AND BARNEY HILL, IN 1966, REVEALS THE DARK SIDE OF UFOLOGY.

The tale of the Hills has become almost folkloric since it was first published in 1966. At the time, it shook ufology to its foundations. This was pretty much the first occasion where the inhabitants of flying saucers—who had so far appeared benign—were abducting humans and subjecting them to medical examinations. The events of this case took place in September 1961,

RIGHT: *While driving along US Route 3 in September 1961, Betty and Barney witnessed a UFO and experienced missing time. Later, during hypnosis, the couple reported being abducted into a UFO by the road at White Mountains, New Hampshire (inset).*

but it was not until after hypnotherapy and regression revealed its details that the story was published.

The Hills were a mixed-race couple from Portsmouth, New Hampshire—Barney, a 39-year-old postal worker; Betty, a 41-year-old social worker. On September 19, 1961, they were returning home from a vacation in Canada when their attention

was caught by a very bright light in the sky. When they pulled over for a closer look, Barney realized that the light, now hovering just above the tree line, was in fact a craft, about 50 feet away and approaching him fast. He even saw humanoid entities peering at him from what seemed to be portholes in the side of the pancake-shaped vehicle. "Gripped with fear," he ran back to the car and sped

ABOVE: *Betty and Barney Hill's case was publicized by John Fuller in the book* The Interrupted Journey *and remains one of the best documented and compelling cases in ufology.*

off. Despite hearing a series of buzzing and beeping sounds, and feeling drowsy, the drive home seemed uneventful. However, by the time they reached Portsmouth it was five in the morning – two hours later than they had expected to arrive.

From then on, the couple – and Barney particularly – began to experience personality changes. Betty started having nightmares of being kidnapped by aliens, and Barney developed symptoms of mental stress, requiring psychiatric treatment. This soon led to a course in hypnotic regression for the Hills, which established what exactly had happened.

Two years after the event, the story emerged. A group of humanoid entities had blocked the road and abducted the Hills into their spacecraft. Both were then subjected to a thorough medical examination, and Betty was shown a star map pinpointing their captors' home planet. This three-

dimensional map was later remodeled by a schoolteacher using beads and string, and researchers making a leap of faith concluded that it most closely matched the Zeta Reticuli star system, almost forty light years from Earth.

As with most cases, there were problems. After the event, Betty became a voracious reader of UFO books, which might have implanted ideas that resurfaced during hypnosis. The star map was refuted by various professional astronomers. And, at the time, the problems of hypnotic regression were little understood. Regardless of such details, the case came to define the abduction experience and opened the floodgates for thousands of other abductees who had their own stories to tell.

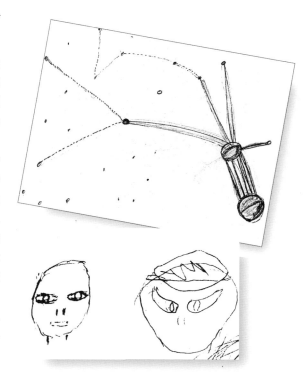

ABOVE: *During hypnosis, Betty Hill drew some sketches of what she experienced. Among these were images of a "star map" showing the aliens' home planet, and the aliens themselves.*

The abduction phenomenon

IN THE YEARS SINCE THE CLASSIC HILLS CASE, THE CLAIMS OF ABDUCTEES WORLDWIDE RETAIN MANY OF THE SAME BASIC ELEMENTS. WHAT EXACTLY MIGHT THIS MEAN—AND WHAT ARE THESE ELEMENTS?

The whole abduction phenomenon has been reported in similar ways by peoples of every race, creed, and psychophysiology. Whether this points to the universality of the aliens' abduction campaign, or to neurologically imbalanced people displaying the same mental characteristics, the experience can be broken down into an almost standard eight-stage sequence of events.

ABOVE: *The consistency of descriptions of aliens during abductions could suggest a real, universal experience.*

1 **PERCEPTION OF UFO OR ALIEN PRESENCE** The experiencer becomes aware of a UFO or an alien being. This is often accompanied by physical effects, such as electromagnetic interference.

2 **BOARDING THE UFO** Although this stage is sometimes not recalled, it is at least implied. Those who do recall claim that they are guided, often by levitation or via some kind of "tractor beam," into the UFO.

3 **PERCEPTION OF INTERIOR** Do all aliens use the same interior designer? Cleanliness, simplicity, and brightness are most often reported.

4 **PERCEPTION OF OCCUPANTS** Once on board, subjects can fully discern their captors, who are most often reported as being of the "Gray" persuasion (*see pages* 80–81). There are various types of entity and a clearly perceived hierarchy. Some witnesses report seeing other abductees.

5 **PHYSICAL EXAMINATION** Subjects usually find themselves naked and are subjected to an examination. This often involves probes that are stuck into navels, penises, or rectums. At this stage, implants may be inserted into an orifice (usually the nose), or under the skin.

ABOVE: *The classic abduction experience of Whitley Strieber was the subject of the book* Communion *and the film of the same name starring Christopher Walken.*

6 **DELIVERY OF MESSAGE** Subjects often initiate conversation with their captors, sometimes telepathically. They are told why they were abducted and often given some kind of profound message that usually reflects contemporary paranoia—nuclear armageddon in the 1960s and '70s; ecological armageddon in the '80s and '90s.

7 **RETURNED TO EARTH** Abductees may receive a tour of the ship. Otherwise, they are returned from whence they came with all but the deepest memories of the event wiped. They only suspect abduction when they perceive a period of missing time—or are told so by a UFO researcher.

8 **AFTEREFFECTS** Subjects notice mental and physical aftereffects, even if they have no recollection. They may seek medical help that unearths the abduction.

THE POWER OF THE MIND

Do all abductees share this set of experiences because we all have one thing in common—the human mind? This theory is supported by research carried out in 1977 by ufologist Dr. Alvin Lawson, which indicated that non-abductees could still "recall" the abduction experience when regressed.

Whichever explanation is correct, the UFO investigator's first task is to deal with the abductee on a human level. Real or otherwise, the abduction experience can be incredibly traumatic, and investigators find themselves in the role of counselor and confidante. Stabilizing the witnesses' mental health should be the first priority, and establishing the background to the case should, at first, involve simply speaking to the witness and building a profile. If possible, avoid the use of hypnotic regression, at least initially. There may be a perfectly mundane explanation for an experience, and this must always be explored before turning to the extraterrestrial hypothesis.

MODERN FOLKLORE

Dr. Thomas "Eddie" Bullard, a folklorist from Indiana University, researched over 250 abduction cases from all over the world in search of parallels between the seemingly set elements of abduction stories and stories from folklore. He concluded that, despite a general similarity, there were enough inherent differences between abduction accounts to assume that they did not share a common origin, as folklore stories do.

Abduction ...
some possible explanations

ACCORDING TO A RECENT SURVEY, AMERICANS ARE MORE LIKELY TO BE ABDUCTED BY ALIENS THAN COMMUTE BY BICYCLE. IS THIS PROOF OF EXTRATERRESTRIALS, OR OF GROWING SCIENTIFIC ILLITERACY?

Approximately two percent of Americans now undergo the classic alien abduction experience—about the same percentage that stutter, live on farms, or suffer physical assault or panic attacks.

My personal belief is that this is largely a twentieth-century psychological phenomenon. Of course, not every abduction report stems from a purely psychological event. Witnessed or mass abductions suggest that there is more to this than mere delusion. However, there are a number of theories that may account for some abduction experiences. Here are some of the major theories that have been put forward:

TEMPORAL LOBE EPILEPSY

Dr. Michael Persinger, a neuroscientist at Laurentian University in Sudbury, Canada, believes that certain patterns of electrical activity in the brain stimulate experiences, one of which is an abduction. Persinger has recreated the sensations of an abduction by stimulating the temporal lobes of the brain. When this stimulation happens naturally, during neurological malfunction, for example, the

ABOVE: *Neuroscientist Dr. Michael Persinger conducting research into temporal lobe epilepsy, one of the possible theories to account for abductions. He believes that electrical brain activity can trigger abduction-effect experiences.*

subject may experience the abduction effect.

One of the main rebuttals against the TLE theory is that, just because the effect can be simulated does not mean that it accounts for it. Persinger says that he can simulate feelings of fear, but this does not mean that fear is not real.

ELECTROSTAGING

English researcher Albert Budden has correlated abduction experiences with sources of electro-magnetic radiation, such as high-tension power cables (left) and areas of tectonic stress. He believes that this radiation triggers an altered state of consciousness, which in turn can trigger an abduction experience.

BIRTH TRAUMA

There is a theory that the medical aspects of abduction—gynecological examination, fetus-like aliens, and the taking of sperm samples—indicate the universal experience of birth. So the abduction experience is in fact a resurfacing of deep-seated memories of this key stage in our development. However, why don't we all experience abductions?

FALSE MEMORY SYNDROME

The mind can suppress traumatic events by mentally sweeping them under a carpet of invented memories. Shreds of these well-buried, invented memories may resurface spontaneously or as a result of hypnosis. Investigators must tread very carefully when exploring this.

TOTAL RECALL

This concept has governments abducting citizens, hypnotizing them, and mind-controlling them to carry out illegal jobs such as assassinations. Then, in order to cover up recall, government spooks implant a memory of abduction, hoping that this will surface during hypnosis.

ASPECTS OF HUMANITY

According to many researchers, aliens are simply part of mythology's roll call, up there with fairies, angels, and demons. In this theory, prevalent in Europe, aliens are archetypes that form a part of the modern collective unconscious.

RIGHT: *A painting of an abduction experience by David Howard, a sufferer of the sleep disorder narcolepsy. With many sleep disorders, the brain cannot tell the difference between the dream world and the real world, and sufferers experience the fantastical as if it were really happening. One of these fantasies is the abduction scenario.*

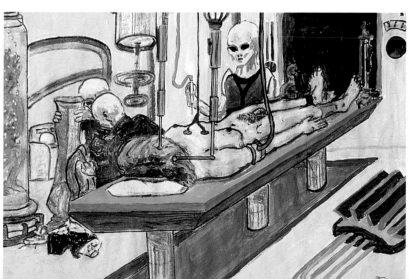

Going back ... hypnotic regression

EVER SINCE IT WAS FIRST USED ON BETTY AND BARNEY HILL, HYPNOTIC REGRESSION HAS PROVED A MOST USEFUL – AND HIGHLY CONTROVERSIAL – TOOL FOR ABDUCTION RESEARCHERS.

In 1963, Barney and Betty Hill contacted Boston psychiatrist Dr. Benjamin Simon to make sense of their bizarre encounter two years earlier on US Highway 3. Simon carried out a series of hypnotic regressions back to the event and initiated the archetypal abduction experience that would be repeated for decades.

Since then, hypnosis has become a much-used ufology tool. "It is the best method available to gain detailed access to people's hidden abduction memories," claims David Jacobs, a history professor from Philadelphia, and one of the major-league ufologists using hypnotic regression today.

Another leading name is artist Budd Hopkins. Following his own UFO sighting in 1964, Hopkins began collating data and, in 1975, investigated his first case. Since then, he has counseled about 2,000 people. Clearly sincere and not driven by any financial goal, Hopkins is adamant that regression hypnosis can be an invaluable tool.

CENTURIES OF SKEPTICISM

The hypnosis phenomenon was first noted by the scientific community in 1784. It was another eighty years before the term hypnosis was used, coined from the Greek hypnos, or "sleep." Since then, hypnotism has been regarded with skepticism and remains on the fringes of science – thanks to the notoriety of stage hypnotists and its occult connections. Its acceptance is further

LEFT: *The alien creatures encountered by abductees Betty and Barney Hill, drawn from testimony provided by the witnesses during controversial hypnotic regression.*

ABOVE: *Parapsychologist Dr. Susan Blackmore is an outspoken critic of alien encounters and the methods of hypnosis used to extract supposedly hidden memories.*

• Dreams can surface during hypnosis, and the saturation of UFO imagery in popular culture means that everyone is susceptible to UFO dreams.

• Ineffectual hypnotists can lead their subject into an alien encounter by asking loaded questions. Try to encourage a complete narrative with simple comments such as "describe what you are seeing."

• A subject's mind often fills in the blanks in their recollections by concocting false memories in order to satisfy the hypnotist.

hindered (unfairly so) by psychic researchers who use it to reveal details of reincarnatees' past lives.

Contrary to the popular notion, hypnotized subjects can still, subconsciously or otherwise, fabricate and embellish their "memories." An actual event and the subject's perceived experiencing of an event can become blurred. Various theories have developed to account for these distortions:

• Hypnotized subjects have been known to speak in the alien language of their "abductors." Most linguistic analyses of such utterances have identified "language types," not actual languages.

• Hypnotized subjects may speak in languages not consciously known to them, probably because the subject has picked up the language subconsciously.

PUTTING HYPNOSIS TO THE TEST

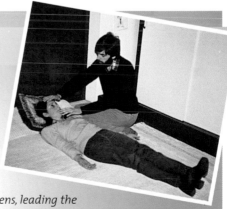

In the 1970s, a team of ufologists and doctors performed "control" experiments at a hospital in California. They advertised for "creative verbal types" who "knew little of and cared less about UFOs." The shortlisted volunteers were then hypnotized and given the suggestion that they had been abducted. The subjects then produced "verbal diarrhea" of levitations, mind probes, examinations, and gray and lizardlike aliens, leading the organizers to conclude that, "ultimately, [alien abduction] was all in the mind."

However, there are some obvious flaws here. For one, the stimulus for the hypnosis came from those controlling the experiment, not as a result of subjects' experiences. The subjects were aware of the test, and probably attempted to satisfy the controllers. Also, the volunteers failed to react physiologically, whereas "real" subjects can visibly quake during regression or suffer years of aftereffects. Ultimately, the volunteers were encouraged to use their imagination – the opposite of what would be expected of "real" abductees.

Hypnosis in action

WHATEVER YOUR OPINION OF HYPNOSIS, IT CAN BE A VALUABLE TOOL –
WHEN UNDERSTOOD AND USED CORRECTLY.

The following is a brief guide as to how hypnosis can be used safely and usefully. It should be stressed that the hypnosis must be carried out by a certified analytical hypnotherapist, not a local ufologist who has simply read a book about it. Take these points on board before you organize hypnosis for any witnesses or undergo it yourself.

ABOVE: *UFO witness Steve Cook took this photograph of his very real experience in 1976. During hypnotic regression to the event, Cook described a "large, gray, saucer-shaped craft" but deeper probing by the qualified therapist revealed that Cook was embellishing the details, despite being hypnotized.*

BEFORE HYPNOSIS

• *Establish that there is a real need for regression. Certain researchers opt for hypnosis only when there is physical proof of an event, or evidence of mental stress (recurring nightmares, irrational fear of a certain stretch of road, etc.)*

• *Once at the hypnotist's place of practice, record all conversations – as all good therapists should also do. Some hypnotists allow investigators to ask questions at the end that can be put to the subject, so keep notes of proceedings. Transcribe all tapes, and add a copy to the subject's file. This account can be compared with the consciously recalled version of events.*

• *The subject will be interviewed before hypnosis to establish their medical history, mental state, dream imagery, and interests – in particular, any interest in ufology and science fiction should be probed.*

• *The therapist should make a final check that the subject is happy to go through with the session, and warn them that the experience may not be pleasant.*

• Hypnotists may attach a simple polygraph lie detector device to the subject to measure their stress levels throughout the session and determine the veracity of their recollections.

• Calming music may be used to induce hypnosis. The therapist may also use visualization during the session to reinforce feelings of relaxation. Later in the session, visualization may also be used to give the subject perspective: seeing the events on a video screen helps to distance the subject and alleviate stressful feelings. Also, they can use their mental remote control to "rewind" or "fast-forward" events.

• The subject should be fed reassurances that nothing is being demanded of them. Subjects who feel under pressure to provide the minutest detail are more likely to fabricate or embellish to satisfy the therapist.

DURING HYPNOSIS

• The subject should be encouraged to provide a chronological narrative of events, but without pressure. They should not be asked specific questions that may "lead" them into false memories.

• Leading questions may be used—but only to establish a subject's susceptibility to suggestion. This is a technique used by Budd Hopkins. During hypnosis, when an "abductee" expressed a fear of rats, Hopkins tried to lead them by saying that he assumed that this was because of their fear of being bitten and catching disease. Instead, the subject claimed it was because they feared the rat climbing their body and staring at them with its big eyes. (This led Hopkins to assume an ET screen memory—a false memory implanted by aliens to mask real events.)

• To check consistency, the therapist may introduce contradictions or ask the same question in a different manner.

• The subject should be continually reassured that they are under no pressure to remember anything.

• Many hypnosis sessions may be required in order to cope fully with a subject's experience. The investigator must not place any pressure on their subject to continue the sessions if they are found too distressing or too revealing. They should also be prepared for the subject to continue working with the therapist privately if another, more personal problem is uncovered.

SUPPORT AT HAND

Subjects who wish to share their experiences can be directed to the many abduction support groups that now operate (see end of book). Alternatively, investigators may wish to organize such support—but should be wary of reinforcing the alien experience in patients who may be suffering from mental illness or delusions. Instead, experiencers should be encouraged to get on with their lives.

Sleep paralysis

HAVE YOU EVER WOKEN UP IN THE NIGHT TERRIFIED, WITH A HEAVY WEIGHT PRESSING ON YOUR CHEST? IF SO, YOU'VE PROBABLY EXPERIENCED SOMETHING THAT MANY PEOPLE REPORT AS AN ALIEN ENCOUNTER ...

"I was overcome ... with terror so fierce and physical that it seemed more biological than psychological. My blood and bones and muscles were much more afraid than my mind. My skin began tingling, my hair felt like it was getting a static charge. The sense of their presence in the room was unimaginably powerful, and so strange. I tried to wake up Anne, but my mouth wouldn't open ..."

These are the words of Whitley Strieber, the world's most famous alien abductee, as he describes the onset of an encounter experience from March 1986. In his bestselling book *Communion*, and a series of sequels, Strieber recounts details of many other similar experiences, his eloquence and erudition placing him in a different league to other abductees.

IT CAN HAPPEN TO ANYONE

Does any of this sound familiar? Have you ever lain in bed—or in your armchair after snoozing—with an overpowering feeling of paralysis, unable to move or cry out? There's a good chance that you have, as these are the sensations experienced during a little-known sleep disorder known as sleep paralysis (SP), and it can happen to anyone, on a scale from mild to truly terrifying.

I'm not for one moment saying that Whitley Strieber is definitely experiencing a simple sleep disorder—his case is a very complex one—but

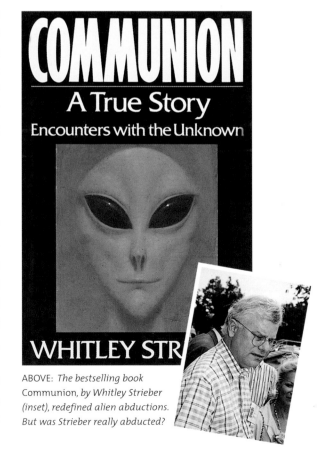

ABOVE: *The bestselling book* Communion, *by Whitley Strieber (inset), redefined alien abductions. But was Strieber really abducted?*

ABOVE: The Nightmare, *an engraving after the painting by Henry Fuseli, depicts the terrifying attack of an incubus, the spirit that attacks—often sexually—in the night. Is this an archaic interpretation of an alien encounter? Or simply a sleep disorder?*

worth knowing something of the mechanism that causes this condition. SP occurs between periods of wakefulness and sleep, and there are two forms. The first emerges as the sufferer falls asleep; the other as the sufferer awakes. In both cases, it appears that the problem occurs because the brain can't make the transition from the dream state to the waking one. A perfectly natural physical paralysis takes place when we sleep, but if we are waking up while this paralysis isn't "turned off" properly, then all kinds of strange sensations can result, including the often-reported one of a heavy weight on the chest. A feature of the waking transitional state is the sensation of floating and hallucinations of orbs of light. Could this account for reports of abductees being "beamed" aboard flying saucers?

there would seem to be a number of similarities between SP and the classic abduction experience. In the seminal *The Terror That Comes in the Night*, for example, author David Hufford describes countless SP cases in which sufferers feel a great weight resting on their chests and experience labored breathing and rapid heartbeat. These symptoms are often accompanied by hallucinations of demons, ghosts, and birds, as well as auditory hallucinations of buzzing, breathing, and footsteps. Some cases even involve acrid smells and the touch of ghostly fingers. Most bizarre of all is the common sighting of an old witch, or mare—the origin of the term "nightmare."

BETWEEN WAKEFULNESS

Given the likelihood that many accounts of abduction will be explained in terms of SP, it is

AWARENESS DURING SP

Sufferers of SP who are conscious of their condition can take control and experience awareness during sleep paralysis (ASP). In this state, experiencers can "direct" the action—similar to those who experiment with lucid dreaming.

To establish the connection between SP and abductions, ASPer Jarno Lahtinen carried out this simple experiment. While experiencing paralysis, he imagined that he was in the early stages of an abduction. "That got my imagination running," he told me. "The wall at the other end of the room started to glow, and I saw a humanoid shape in the middle of the light." Lahtinen was truly terrified of his SP-induced alien visitor, suggesting that his experiences were the same as that of "real" abductees.

Medical evidence

IN CHAPTER 2, WE BROACHED THE SUBJECT OF PHYSICAL EVIDENCE OF SIGHTINGS OF DISTANT OR LANDED UFOs. BUT WHAT OF HUMAN PHYSICAL EVIDENCE THAT COMES FROM ACTUAL ENCOUNTERS?

Take your clothes off and give your body a thorough examination. Are there any scars, scratches, or bruises that you cannot account for? If so, could you have been the victim of an alien abduction …?

According to American abduction researchers David Jacobs and Budd Hopkins, "peculiar incisions, needlelike marks, triangular bruises, and scooplike scars of unknown origin seem to add further 'evidence' as to the existence of some kind of anomalous event." But is there medical evidence to link inexplicable scars to the encounter phenomenon? There follows a run-down of some of the main physical "evidence."

PARALYSIS

Numerous encounter claims, like many sightings claims, have included reports of craft or aliens rendering the witness unconscious or paralyzed by means of a tool or weapon—usually the ubiquitous laser beam. With most cases, there is no physical evidence to investigate, though there may well be mental trauma. It is usually difficult to establish whether paralysis is simply brought on by the witnesses being "frozen" with fear, a half-sleeping daydream state (perhaps SP, *see pages* 74–75) or from alien intent.

PHYSICAL SCARRING

According to US ufologist Derrel Sims, otherwise undetectable scars received during abductions—supposedly caused by probing or tissue biopsy—can be revealed under ultraviolet light. Science can do little to authenticate claims, except possibly to judge when the scars were formed.

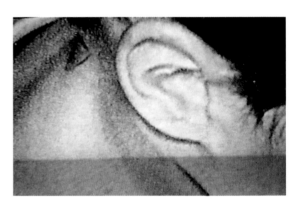

ABOVE: *Scars and gouge-marks—such as the triangular wound on this alleged abductee—are often discovered on the bodies of those who have had alien experiences.*

PHANTOM PREGNANCY

Many abduction cases investigated by New Yorker Budd Hopkins feature women who claim to have lost fetuses to their alien captors. Hopkins is convinced that aliens are abducting

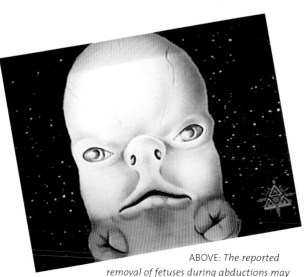

ABOVE: *The reported removal of fetuses during abductions may be carried out in order to create alien-human hybrids, such as this "star-child" (artist's impression).*

women in order to artificially inseminate them. The aliens then re-abduct the "host" weeks or months later and retrieve the growing fetus.

"Kathie Davis," who is featured in Hopkins' book, *Intruders*, was supposedly abducted and impregnated in 1977. Following another abduction in 1978, the fetus was said to have been removed. Similar events have occurred since, some of them resulting in the appearance of physical evidence.

DEATH

While animals are apparently killed and mutilated by UFOs by their dozen, there have been no reliable reports of humans being murdered by aliens. There are, however, cases in which alleged contact with extraterrestrial entities was followed by death.

In 1967, when Brazilian plantation manager Inácio de Souza encount-

ered three aliens, he unslung his carbine and shot at them. As he did so, he was struck down by a beam fired from their flying-saucer. Two months later, he was dead. The death of British engineer Kenneth Edwards has been attributed to his alien encounter. Edwards was driving past an Atomic Energy Authority plant when a silver-suited being fired a laser bolt at him. After the event, he became lethargic and his kidneys failed. After four years of pain, he died. Both men died from cancer.

Did the victims die because of their encounter, or was the cancer present beforehand? One theory is that cancers cause hallucinations, or subconscious imagery, that alert the sufferer to the fact that they have the disease – a common occurrence in paranormal circles whereby unsuspecting "sensitives" receive visions of an illness that is later confirmed by doctors.

BELOW: *On May 20, 1968, amateur geologist Stephen Michalak was prospecting in Falcon Lake, Manitoba, when he witnessed the landing of a strange craft. On approaching it, hot air blasted out of a ventilation grill, leaving Michalak with first-degree burns. He also reported severe vomiting and diarrhea, skin infections, and swelling of his joints – a prognosis confirmed by the 27 doctors who treated him.*

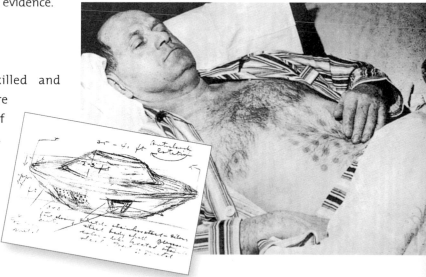

Implants

ARE ALIENS IMPLANTING HUMAN ABDUCTEES WITH MIND-CONTROL OR MONITORING DEVICES? IF NOT, WHAT ARE THE STRANGE METALLIC OBJECTS FOUND IN THE BODIES OF ALLEGED ABDUCTEES?

On August 19, 1995, Derrel Sims—UFO researcher, former CIA member, and certified medical hypnotherapist—took part in ground-breaking surgery to remove what he believes is an alien artefact implanted into an abductee. In the operation, Sims and surgeon Dr. Roger Leir removed two small metallic objects from the right big toe of the middle-aged female patient. The entire procedure was videoed and relayed live via a monitor to an audience in an adjoining antechamber. After the surgery, a second alleged abductee came forward and also had a small object excised, this time from his hand.

The objects in question appeared to be attached to the patients' nerves, and all proved difficult to extract. Ranging in size from 4.1 millimeters to 5.75 millimeters, the "implants" appeared metallic and covered in a tough organic coating. These characteristics were confirmed when samples were sent for further professional analysis. Tests also revealed that the objects had a mainly iron core (strengthened with carbon) with a coating composed of iron, calcium, phosphorus, and chlorine.

This may sound impressive, but the tests failed to confirm anything extraterrestrial about the objects—leading critics to denounce them as unnoticed or long-forgotten splinters, or even a natural product of the body. But remember that just because objects are composed of elements

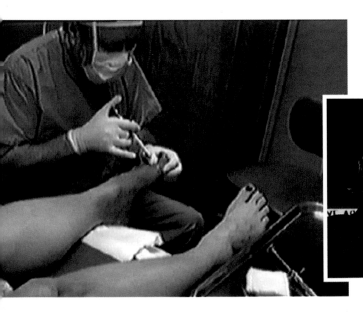

FAR LEFT: *Dr. Roger Leir and Derrel Sims (right) perform the extraction of an alleged alien implant from the foot of an abductee.*

LEFT: *Former CIA agent Sims, the self-appointed "Alien Hunter," began his research after his own alien encounter. He has focused his efforts on physical evidence and hopes one day to catch an alien during the act of abduction.*

available on Earth does not mean that they're not extraterrestrial in origin.

VICTIM TESTIMONY

The idea of implantation is not inconceivable—farmers have been known to implant animals with minute location-finding devices, but the only

ABOVE: *Derrel Sims has collected numerous samples of physical evidence for alien encounters, many of which he believes are alien implants that may be used for tracking or mind control.*

evidence that this is taking place in humans is victim testimony—on which the investigator can't rely too heavily. In addition, the simplicity of the

objects so far extracted makes it difficult to accept that they serve any special purpose.

David Pritchard, physicist at the Massachusetts Institute of Technology, is one of the few qualified researchers willing to address the issue of implantation seriously. He believes that the key is to find some correlation between anomalous foreign bodies and alleged abductees. If the occurrences of such objects are higher in a sample of abductees than in a non-abductee sample, it would lend credence to the theory that aliens are taking part in some campaign to tag humans. (Of course, who's to say that the non-abductees just haven't realized they've been space-napped?)

No one denies, as such, the existence of such "alien" objects. There is enough X-ray, video, and lab evidence to confirm that inexplicable foreign bodies find their way into human bodies, but exactly what they are is open to question. The only thing you can do as an investigator is to get them out of the body and into a lab for analysis—but be prepared to file the findings in your "gray basket."

EXTRACTING IMPLANTS

What should you do when approached by an alleged implantee? Again, it comes down to who you can turn to for assistance. Don't try amateur electromagnetic photography or kitchen-table surgery. Find a qualified medical practitioner who can provide X-rays of the suspected implant and a referral to a surgeon.

Many of the larger UFO groups have medical experts on stand-by for such situations, while university hospitals may also offer assistance. The most important thing is to have qualified surgeons undertake the work, not just anyone with a background in medicine. When it comes to convincing the scientists, you can't afford to be perfunctory.

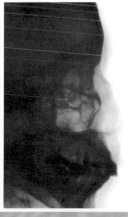

ABOVE: *An X-ray of abductee Linda Cortile revealed an alleged nasal implant. The implant later vanished before it could be removed.*

What do aliens look like?

IT SEEMS THAT EARTH IS BEING VISITED BY MANY DIFFERENT TYPES OF ALIEN—
LIFE IN THE UNIVERSE APPEARS TO BE AS DIVERSE AS IT IS ON OUR PLANET. WHAT
DOES THIS TELL YOU ABOUT WITNESSES' TESTIMONY?

Leading American ufologist Patrick Huyghe has collected hundreds of reports of aliens seen during close encounters. From this, he devised a classification system based on their phenotype (observable characteristics). Huyghe has simplified his system to four Classes, subdivided into several Types, and then into Variants. When questioning a witness about alien encounters, keep in mind his system. Gather as much descriptive/sketched detail as possible and ask them to place their entity into one of the categories.

ABOVE: *Patrick Huyghe, co-publisher of* Anomalist *magazine, who has devised a classification system for aliens.*

HUMANOID

This class, the largest in the system, is devoted to aliens with the "same basic body plan as the human." Distinguishing features are cylindrical trunk with one head, and two legs and arms attached at shoulders and hips respectively.

HUMAN *These are humanoids that are all but indistinguishable from human beings. The most famous examples include the alien met by George Adamski, who was tall, blonde, beautiful, and "Nordic." Variants include those in space suits, and older, wrinkled aliens (popularly known as Elders).*

SHORT GRAYS *The most famous aliens, the Short Grays are the stars of Spielberg's film* Close Encounters of the Third Kind *and are the space-nappers of celebrated abductees Whitley Strieber and Betty and Barney Hill. They are usually no taller than five feet and have recognizably alien features such as strangely colored (but not necessarily gray) skin, and large, wraparound or almond-shaped eyes.*

SHORT NON-GRAYS *Short humanoids that vary significantly from the oft-reported grays have their own category. These are the "little green men" of*

1950s fiction, or humanoids too small or hairy to be classed in any other category.

GIANT This self-explanatory category is reserved for the larger non-human humanoids—those of five feet and above. Variants include those with single and multiple eyes.

NON-CLASSIC This is the humanoid catch-all category. Notable within this class are the five-foot-tall "elephant-skinned" beings that abducted fishermen Charles Hickson and Calvin Parker from the banks of the Pascagoula River, Mississippi, in October 1973.

ABOVE: *Spielberg's film* Close Encounters of the Third Kind *popularized the classic, almond-eyed gray alien (also inset). It was thought that reported sightings of these aliens would rise after the film but, surprisingly, this was not the case.*

RIGHT: *The humanoid human encountered by Adamski in his desert rendezvous with the unknown.*

ANIMALIAN

The second largest class is animalian, and according to Huyghe includes "anything that's hairy, scaly, moves on four legs, or has wings."

HAIRY MAMMALIAN *Distinguished by their covering of hair. Variants include Bigfoot, the huge beast seen by the Pulaski family in Greensburg, Pennsylvania, in 1973.*

REPTILIAN *These reptilelike entities include the silvery, glowing beings (right) that besieged the Sutton family farm near Hopkinsville, Kentucky, on August 21–22, 1955.*

AMPHIBIAN *These actually have no connection with water. They include froglike aliens and those with eyes on stalks, as in the headless entities said to have abducted Massachusetts housewife Betty Andreasson.*

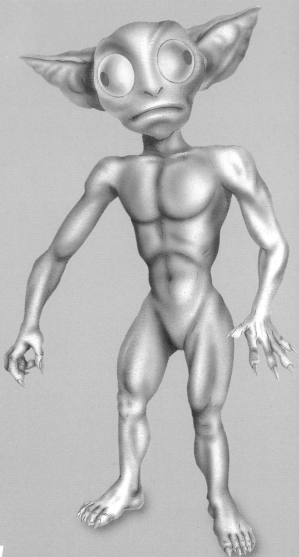

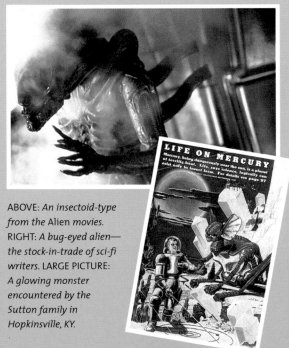

ABOVE: *An insectoid-type from the* Alien *movies.* RIGHT: *A bug-eyed alien— the stock-in-trade of sci-fi writers.* LARGE PICTURE: *A glowing monster encountered by the Sutton family in Hopkinsville, KY.*

INSECTOID *Animalians with insect features: multiple eyes and/or legs, spindly appendages, and sets of wings. Also includes a variety that could be classed as "fairies," owing to their rounded wings.*

AVIAN *A category reserved for aliens with bird- or bat-like wings. The mothman—a headless, six-foot-tall creature with batwings—terrorized numerous witnesses in England in the 1960s.*

ROBOTIC

Aliens of a mechanical nature are classed as robotic. In addition to the classic, Metropolislike sci-fi robot, this also includes non-humanoid robots that often resemble mechanical or electrical devices.

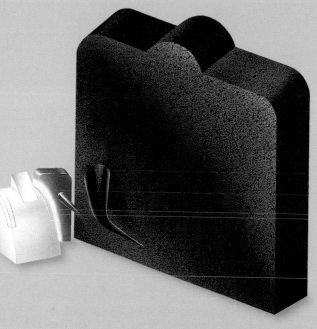

METALLIC *Variants include those with a metallic or metallike skin. The most famous examples are the "Mines" that attacked Scots forester Robert Taylor in 1979.*

FLESHY *Androit-like entities with recognizably organic features such as areas of fleshy or scaly skin. Robotics with humanoid features are also included in this category.*

ABOVE: *In 1977 witness Lee Parrish joined three machinelike beings in their UFO in Kentucky. The largest was twenty feet high and shaped like a tombstone with one handless "arm."*

EXOTIC

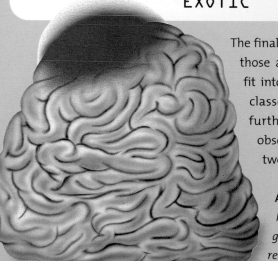

The final class incorporates those aliens that do not fit into any of the other classes. Huyghe has further divided these obscure entities into two types.

APPARITIONAL *In-corporeal or ghostlike extra-terrestrials, or those* *that appear only partly formed. This type could also encompass spirit entities.*

PHYSICAL *The final catch-all type for the entire system, this category houses anything physical but without humanoid, animalian, or robotic features. Of particular note is the twenty-inch-tall, bluish "brain" that communicated with two men in California in 1971.*

Come on in ... close encounters of the fifth kind

A RECENT ADDITION TO HYNEK'S CLASSIFICATION SYSTEM IS CEV, OR CLOSE ENCOUNTERS OF THE FIFTH KIND – A CATEGORY RESERVED FOR THOSE UNIQUE CASES IN WHICH HUMANS ACTIVELY SEEK OUT AND MAKE CONTACT WITH ETs.

Whereas the contactees of the 1950s claimed that they were singled out by aliens for communication between the stars, by the 1990s, a bizarre new twist had developed – humans are now seeking out the aliens.

This human-initiated contact, or Close Encounter of the Fifth Kind, can take many forms. However, the overall idea is to open a channel of communication – be it telepathically, electronically, or otherwise – to any extraterrestrial intelligence who may be listening. The ultimate goal is to board an alien spacecraft as part of a diplomatic rendezvous.

LEFT: *Dale E. Graff, the former head of Project Stargate, the US military's 20-year remote viewing project. The project underwent many changes of name and objective, and it has been suggested that one of the aims was to psychic-spy on aliens and UFOs. This form of CEV can also be attempted by keen ufologists.*

IS ANYBODY OUT THERE?

The principal organization offering this interstellar olive branch is the North Carolina-based Center for the Study of Extraterrestrial Intelligence (CSETI). Fronted by emergency physician Dr. Steven Greer, CSETI's goal is to "precipitate or facilitate a landing, with mental concentration and then a conscious meeting with these visitors." Many members from the group's twenty-five branches throughout the world have claimed certain degrees of success, usually as the result of spending a night skywatching and willing the visitors to appear.

For the modern ufologist, the sort of activity involved in stimulating a CEV provides much-needed active participation, an aspect of ufology sorely lacking. As far as I am concerned, if ufology is your hobby, then why not take an active part in it – what have you got to lose from sitting all night in a field, other than body heat? You never know what you may find.

So, for those of you with an inclination to meet our space brothers, the list on the opposite page provides possible techniques for attracting alien attention. Be careful, though: who knows what you may encounter...

MAKING CONTACT ... A PROACTIVE GUIDE

From the golden age of flying saucers, ufologists have attempted to make contact with the inhabitants or pilots of UFOs. To some, this is a futile gesture; to others, it is a chance to become more actively involved in the subject. You can make up your own mind with these contact tips:

SKYWATCHING *Pack your lunch box and thermos and wrap up warm. Then head for a UFO hotspot and wait. As silly as this sounds, you simply have a better chance of seeing UFOs if you're looking for them. CSETI also promote meditation during skywatches, and Greer suggests taking along a flashlight, perhaps with colored filters, to help you communicate. Paint light-shapes in the sky with the beam and wait for the response.*

TELEPATHY *Sightings of nocturnal lights are common, but if you witness one, try communicating through telepathy. Simply ask the lights to do something like flash or fly in a circular motion. This is the method of communication employed successfully by the two Norfolk contactees I mentioned earlier (see page 38).*

CHANNELING *If skywatching sounds too much like hard work, you could try channeling aliens. In the same way that spiritualists claim to be able to act as conduits for the Earthly-departed, so too have some contactees supposedly channeled aliens. Evidence for this comes in the form of automatic alien handwriting, and alien speech delivered through the channeler's own mouth.*

REMOTE VIEWING *The US military invested much time and money researching psychic skills as a tool for spying. The project, known latterly as Project Stargate, ended with military psychics remote-viewing the Loch Ness Monster, Atlantis, and aliens. If it worked for them, it might work for you. Courses are available.*

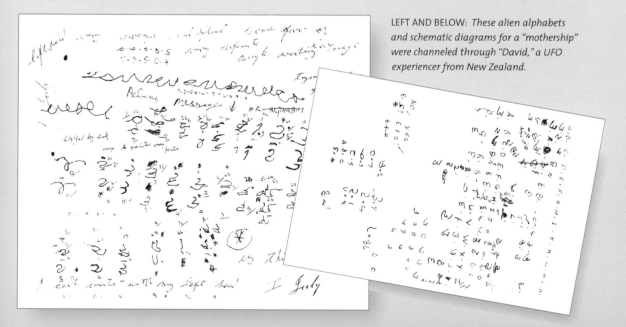

LEFT AND BELOW: *These alien alphabets and schematic diagrams for a "mothership" were channeled through "David," a UFO experiencer from New Zealand.*

Rough guide to Magonia

ONE SCHOOL OF THOUGHT CLAIMS THAT ALIEN PHENOMENA ARE SIMPLY MODERN FOLKLORE, AND WITNESSES AND ABDUCTEES ARE MERELY EXPERIENCING THE SAME EPISODES AS PEOPLE LONG AGO REPORTED ENCOUNTERS WITH FAIRIES AND TROLLS.

There is a place in the sky where the locals are a strange population of fairies, wizards, religious icons, and aliens ... oh, and everyone speaks Latin. The name of this region is Magonia, and you can take a trip there any time.

"Magonian" is the term now adopted by a certain school of ufology to describe the many manifestations of the UFO phenomenon. The word has its roots in a ninth-century manuscript in which Archbishop Agobard of Lyon, France, links anti-Christian superstitions of the day with a mythical island called Magonia. Magonia has since been adopted to house the ever-growing dramatis personae of mythology and folklore—and the latest arrivals are the extraterrestrial creatures and their magical craft (perhaps there are drinking bars on Magonia patronized by the weirdest-looking collection of "cloud ship" captains, wizards, fairies, and aliens—something like the cantina scene from *Star Wars*).

VALLEE'S HYPOTHESIS

One of the first modern ufologists to turn his attention to Magonia was influential French astrophysicist Jacques Vallee. After analyzing statistical models drawn from countless UFO and abduction reports, Vallee concluded that the "physical and spiritual constants of the UFO phenomenon could be traced to the folklore of every culture."

While not totally rejecting the extraterrestrial hypothesis, Vallee believes that there has been a "control system" exerted on us since the dawn of humanity: "During the period of antiquity, the wheels of Ezekiel, cherubim, and burning bushes were observed .... During the nineteenth century,

LEFT: *Some of Magonia's oldest inhabitants are the fairies, the "little people" who were reported in the past in the same way that aliens are reported today. Both aliens and fairies can be seen as being figments of our imagination or collective unconscious.*

phantom airships were seen ... and today there are reports of spacecraft."

Before Vallee, the Swiss psychotherapist Carl Jung had quietly summarized his own impartial feelings on the UFO phenomenon in his perceptive book, *Flying Saucers: a Modern Myth of Things Seen in the Sky* (1958). And today, the British magazine *Magonia*, which explores the folkloric aspects of ufology with open-mindedness and humor, is still in circulation since its launch in 1968.

COUNTER-ARGUMENTS

Veteran ufologist Jerome Clark points out the most obvious flaw in the folklore theory: "the psychosocial hypothesis simply fails to deal with ufology's most interesting questions, the ones that brought it into being in the first place: namely, those related to physical evidence, instrumented observations ... and independently witnessed events."

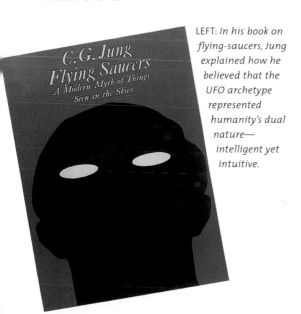

LEFT: *In his book on flying-saucers, Jung explained how he believed that the UFO archetype represented humanity's dual nature—intelligent yet intuitive.*

NEW DIMENSIONS

Various researchers have tried to synthesize the extraterrestrial and psychosocial hypotheses into a unified theory, one that accounts for both the physical and psychological evidence for UFOs. Psychologist Michael Grosso believes that UFOs originate in the "ultradimensional mind"—a kind of parallel universe formed by the collective unconscious. UFOs are, he suggests, psychic projections from this mental universe that can influence radar. Another recently coined term, cyberbiology, defines the mind's ability to interact with external systems—producing the physical manifestation of entities we know as aliens.

Psychologist Kenneth Ring (above inset) takes this further by suggesting that "psychoterrestrial" entities exist in a "Third Kingdom," similar to Magonia, that can be accessed via an altered state of consciousness. When someone has a UFO experience, they are merely slipping into this world, or opening up a gateway that allows the inhabitants to enter our world.

THE SIXTH WAY

Just when you thought you could count the types of encounter on one hand, along comes Close Encounters of the Sixth Kind (CEVIs). These are cases in which humans have become possessed by the spirits of aliens and require the services of a specialized alien "exorcist."

CHAPTER FOUR

Analysis

Nothing in life is to be feared.
It is only to be understood.

MARIE CURIE

Here we turn our attention to UFOs on film—both stills and moving footage—and just how far they help us analyze the phenomenon. Since the invention of the camera, thousands of photographs showing UFOs have been taken. Yet, how often have you heard—or asked—the question: "If UFOs exist, why are there no decent photos of them?" The problem is twofold. First, witnesses to most types of spectacular phenomena rarely have a camera on hand. Second, almost anything can look like a flying saucer if it is photographed in the appropriate manner.

COMPELLING EVIDENCE

Despite this rather unfair view, the camera has provided compelling evidence in support of the extraterrestrial hypothesis. There are many cases in the hundred-year history of the UFO photograph in which analysis has proved that the object photographed is a large, structured object in the sky. These cases are very difficult to dispute and are often ignored by cynics.

MAIN PICTURE: *The photographs of the flying saucers at Gulf Breeze, Florida, are among the best and most contested of all UFO imagery. So just how much can we trust photographic and video evidence for UFOs when it seems as if the best photographs are the most unbelievable? Fortunately, technology—and common sense—is at hand to guide us.*

The 1990s have seen an explosion of camcorder UFO evidence. The availability of this technology has resulted in ufologists being flooded by tapes of poorly filmed flying objects. Some footage, though—such as these black triangle UFOs filmed over Norfolk, England, in 1998—leaves little to the imagination.

Cloud? Aircraft? Flying saucer? According to the photographer—who snapped the image at the Museum of the Horse in New Mexico in January 1996—there was nothing in the sky when the photograph was taken. This is typical of many UFO images: taken alone, they are more or less worthless; if offered to support an eyewitness account, their value increases ... but how much?

Pictures may paint a thousand words, but how many of them are lies? As the ridiculous seance photographs of the Victorian era proved, charlatans have been able to fake photographs since the invention of the camera. Like many other UFO images, this one from 1966 is a fake. But how can you tell?

Ufology ... A history in photos

THE HISTORY OF THE UFO PHOTOGRAPH IS AN INTRIGUING ONE AND SHOWS THAT SOME WITNESSES DO SUCCEED IN CAPTURING ON FILM BIZARRE OBJECTS THAT CAN'T BE PUT DOWN TO MERE CAMERA FAULTS OR NATURAL PHENOMENA.

The first UFO witness to provide photographic proof of their sighting was José A. Y. Bonilla, Director of the Observatory of Zacatecas in Mexico. On August 12, 1883, Bonilla was using a telescope camera to shoot sunspots, when a number of objects passed in front of the Sun. One of these objects—"a five-pointed star with a dark center"— paused long enough to be photographed before "regrouping" with its companions.

Confirmation of the objects came from observatories in Mexico City and Puebla, discrediting theories that Bonilla snapped fireflies or migrating geese. Bonilla himself believed the objects to be passing by the Earth near the Moon, but refused to speculate on what they might have been. However, the debate as to the identity of the objects was underway—a debate that continues to this day.

HAZY HISTORY

For the next fifty years, UFOs continued to be photographed. Notable examples include one of "Foo Fighters," the balls of light that pilots reported buzzing their planes. But in most of the photographs from this period, the subjects were hazy and could really have been anything.

However, a series of photographs taken in 1950 defied the sceptics. Paul Trent and his wife, farmers in McMinnville, Oregon, witnessed UFO activity over their farm and photographed one of the objects. American astronomer William Hartmann, a government-appointed UFO investigator, concluded: "This is one of the few UFO reports in which all factors investigated, geometric, psychological, and physical, appear to be consistent with the assertion that an extraordinary flying object, silvery, metallic, disk-shaped, tens of yards in diameter, and evidently artificial, flew within sight of two witnesses."

ABOVE: *A World War II Tachikawa Ki 36 is buzzed by a "foo fighter" ball of light UFO. This is a rare photograph of the foo phenomenon that was taken in 1942.*

ABOVE: *One of the two McMinnville photographs, which have proved the most enduring of all UFO photographs.*

Analysis confirmed that the object was about one hundred feet wide, but that it was shot in the morning, not in the evening as claimed. Despite this, this image is most convincing evidence.

ENTER ADAMSKI

More controversial UFO photographs were taken two years later by "Reverend" and "Professor" George Adamski. Most of Adamski's images were shot using a plate-camera attached to a Tinsley telescope and show domed, disk-shaped craft and a "mothership" from which "scoutcraft" emerge.

For most critics, the photos really are "too good to be true," yet attempts to discredit them have failed. Adamski himself offered $2,000 to anyone who could prove that the images were faked, yet no one was confident enough to accept his offer. Instead, critics focus on the fact that Venus, and other planets supposedly visited by Adamski, are inhospitable.

THE VILLA STORY

Another series of controversial photographs was that of Paul Villa. Ten years after his first contact with aliens in 1953, Villa began snapping pictures of saucer-shaped craft with his Apus folding camera. If some of the images look like they're of models, this is because some are. Villa admitted to building a three-foot-diameter model, but claimed that the specifications came from his "space friends."

Investigation and digital analysis revealed the Villa shots to be fakes, although William Sherwood, an optical physicist for Eastman-Kodak, concluded after his own research that they were genuine. As these two conflicting "expert analyses" show, the investigation of UFO photographs is as open to subjectivity as any other aspect of the UFO phenomenon.

Gulf Breeze ... a case in point

A SIMILAR STALEMATE HAS BEEN REACHED BETWEEN INVESTIGATORS INVOLVED IN THE INFAMOUS GULF BREEZE CASE IN FLORIDA.

In November 1987, a man known only as "Mr. Ed" reported a UFO encounter and backed it up with a series of photographs. Over the next few years, Mr. Ed—later revealed to be Mr. Ed Walters from the Pensacola Bay area—continued to witness UFO activity, all of which was recorded on film.

GROWING BODY OF EVIDENCE

Unlike most photographic cases, however, the Gulf Breeze phenomenon does not stop at Ed Walters. Many residents and visitors to the area have since taken their own photographs and video footage of large, structured craft or anomalous lights in the sky. This is what makes Gulf Breeze such a compelling case. Not only are there multiple witnesses, but they are all taking photographs. Some are even using Polaroid cameras (the prints from which are notoriously difficult, although not impossible, to tamper with), and others are using sealed three-dimensional or stereoscopic cameras.

Despite this, all was not as it seemed. A UFO model, suspiciously similar to one photographed by Walters, was found in his attic, and a local man admitted to helping him fake shots. At around the same time, pranksters thought it would be fun to launch mini hot-air balloons and helium balloons. The Pensacola skies suddenly became crowded—

THE ALEX BIRCH HOAX

While the camera has revolutionized the investigation of UFOs, it has also been a thorn in the ufologist's side. One good example is that of Alex Birch, the teenager who in 1962 presented Britain with one of its best UFO photos. The image shows a fleet of saucers over Sheffield, England, and was so convincing at the time that Birch was invited to speak at the inaugural meeting of the British UFO Research Association.

After ten years, Birch confessed that his picture merely showed blobs of paint daubed on a sheet of glass. Of course, we can look back now and scoff at such a poor attempt at fakery. Back then, though, this kind of image was just what UFO research groups wanted to draw the crowds, and researchers hungrily snapped it up. If nothing else, though, Birch at least heralded the introduction of strict codes of practice for the investigation of UFO images and taught ufologists not to believe everything that they are told—or shown—by witnesses.

LEFT, ABOVE & TOP LEFT: *A series of images taken by Ed Walters at Gulf Breeze. After more than ten years, Walters and many of the multiple witnesses still stick to their original stories. Some ufologists believe that it is still too early to pass judgment on the Gulf Breeze case, although it seems that the tide may be turning against the witnesses.*

and so too did the area, as ufologists made a pilgrimage to the resort. (I must confess to having mischievously flown a stunt kite at Gulf Breeze with a friend; no one fell for it, as far as we know.)

IS NO ONE TO BE TRUSTED?

The events at Gulf Breeze continue to this day, and photos continue to be taken—even if some are local kids playing pranks with helium balloons.

Whether or not you believe Ed Walters (he passed a polygraph test, for what it's worth), the official Mutual UFO Network investigation concluded that the case was genuine, despite the locals' attempts at hoaxing. However, it now appears that there is a large-scale conspiracy among locals, and the phenomenon is something of a hoax that got out of hand. Anyway, why not visit the area and see for yourself (*see* Chapter 6) ... just remember to take your camera, and trust no one.

Analyzing UFO photos

WHILE IT IS ALWAYS RECOMMENDED THAT INVESTIGATORS SEND POTENTIAL UFO IMAGES FOR PROFESSIONAL ANALYSIS, SAVE TIME AND MONEY BY ELIMINATING OBVIOUS FAKES BEFOREHAND WITH A FEW SIMPLE TESTS OF YOUR OWN.

One of the most fundamental problems with UFO imagery is that what the eye sees, the brain interprets as something it understands. Take the famous "Face on Mars" photograph that allegedly showed a sculpted face in the Cydonia region. It looked like a face, but that did not mean it was a face. This was borne out by the re-surveying of the planet in 1998, which proved that the original image was merely a trick of the light.

USING YOUR HOME COMPUTER

While the brain may be fooled, the computer is less easy to trick and can be a valuable ally in investigating UFO images. The basic kit for photo (and to a lesser extent video) analysis consists of a middle-range desktop computer (PC or Macintosh), a flat-bed scanner, and, for video, a video player that can be connected to the computer.

Simply scan prints into the computer (at the highest possible resolution) and use image-manipulation software to carry out an analysis. In the case of videos, stills and sequences can be obtained using special "video-grabbing" software.

Where possible, return to the area where the images were taken and shoot your own series of images or footage from the same spot. These can be used for later reference by a professional analyst.

Also, measure the distances between yourself and objects in the shots such as buildings and trees, and try to estimate the UFO's position. This will help the analyst determine the geometry and lighting of the scene, and help in judging the size of the UFO.

Where relevant, always demand negatives in order to rule out processing problems. Once you're satisfied that the UFO is not a processing flaw, use your computer for a more detailed study. If you are then satisfied that the image is worthy of further tests, it should undergo professional analysis.

PIXELLATION Check that prints are "first generation" by enlarging any area. If the image is pixellated, it will have been scanned into a computer and may have been manipulated. Examine the pixelation of the UFO and background to make sure it matches.

LIGHTING Does light hit the object from the same angle that it hits surrounding objects? Boost shadows by altering variables such as brightness and contrast, or check color contouring to confirm the three-dimensionality of the object.

FOCUS The number of pixels on the objects' edges will indicate how much they are in focus. Objects with the same degree of focus can be expected to be the same distance from the camera.

This photographic print was sent to me anonymously in May 1998. Nothing was known about the image, so computer analysis was used to decide whether or not the image was worthy of professional—and costly—analysis. After analysis, detailed below, it was decided that no further assessment was necessary.

"AUTO-ADJUST" FILTER *This built-in function looks for the darkest and lightest areas, turns them to black and white respectively, and adjusts the intermediate shades accordingly. This increases the tonal range of the image, aiding the identification of badly lit subjects.*

"EMBOSS" FILTER *Identifies high-contrast edges and offers the user the ability to raise or sink elements by a given number of pixels. This embosses objects in the image, helping to distinguish between solid objects and those that are two-dimensional.*

"UNSHARP MASK" FILTER *Compensates for images that were photographed slightly out of focus. It increases the contrast between neighboring pixels on the "threshold" (edge of an object) and/or "radius" (overall image), but cannot correct very out-of-focus images.*

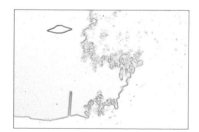

"FIND EDGES" FILTER *This traces around pixels, accentuating the edges and outlining shapes and colors. Useful for identifying elements such as string or thread that may otherwise be invisible to the naked eye.*

"COLOR CONTOURING/PSEUDOCOLOR" *Attributes false colors to areas with a similar light intensity. Helps to pick out light or dark objects against areas of highlight or shadow, and to identify 3-D objects.*

"CONTRAST AND BRIGHTNESS" *Compensates for images shot in limited or excessive light by altering the degree of difference between the dark and light elements within the shot.*

Moving pictures ...
UFOs on film

THE UFO HAS APPEARED IN MOVIES—FILM, VIDEO, OR DIGITAL STOCK—FOR ALMOST HALF A CENTURY. YOU WOULD EXPECT MOVING IMAGES TO FORM IRREFUTABLE EVIDENCE, BUT THEY ARE JUST AS OPEN TO INTERPRETATION AS ANY OTHER FORM.

In September 1991, above western Australia, video cameras mounted on the space shuttle *Discovery* recorded a flurry of UFO activity near the Earth's horizon. A small, bright object, among the many ice crystals also visible, is seen drifting through space. Suddenly, there is a flash of light, and the object immediately changes direction and starts heading out into space. Another object, traveling at a great speed, streaks through the camera's field of vision and joins the first object.

This incredible footage is one of many NASA videos displaying compelling evidence for the reality of ET craft. NASA claims that the objects in the *Discovery* video are merely ice crystals, although how ice crystals in space can change direction so rapidly is anyone's guess.

THE GREAT FALLS MOVIE

One of the very first pieces of film evidence was shot on August 15, 1950, in the Legion Ball Park in Montana, home of the Selectrics baseball team. The team's general manager, Nicholas Mariana, and his secretary witnessed two bright, 50-foot-wide objects "like two new dimes." Using his 16-mm movie camera, Mariana filmed the objects for 16 seconds, capturing about 315 frames.

Following a newspaper report, Air Force Office of Special Investigation took the film for analysis. "The Air Force has no interest in the film," researchers claimed, and returned the film to Mariana. However, Mariana discovered that the beginning of the reel, showing the two disks spinning, was now gone. The Air Force denied everything.

ADAMSKI RIDES AGAIN

Film evidence from contactees such as George Adamski and Howard Menger dominated the remainder of the 1950s and 1960s, over-

LEFT: *A still from George Adamski's film, known as the "Silver Springs" film, shot in 1965 on an 8-mm camera.*

occurring over Mexico City since 1991. Heralded by the solar eclipse on July 11, that year, UFO activity has become commonplace in the largest metropolis on the planet. During the eclipse, seventeen people filmed the same metallic object for half an hour. Once news of this appeared on TV, hundreds of hours of footage showing UFO activity during and after the eclipse flooded in.

FILE UNDER GRAY AREA

There has been no single case that stands up on footage alone, perhaps because there's something about alien craft that prevents them from being seen clearly on film, or the objects recorded are merely aircraft or natural phenomena, or flawed cameras have been used. All that researchers can do is analyze the footage and be prepared to file findings in the "unknowns" tray.

ABOVE: *Among hundreds of hours of footage filmed throughout Mexico since 1991 is this intriguing few minutes captured by Guillermo Osorio in January 1996. Osorio was not the only observer: many of his neighbors and others across the town of Puebla were also witness to the slow-moving streaks. Initial theories that the objects were meteors entering the atmosphere were ruled out by computer analysis (inset pictures).*

shadowing other witnesses. However, there is one piece of Adamski film evidence that continues to stir controversy. The "Silver Springs" film shows a "flying saucer" performing a series of maneuvers. The saucer also appears to warp. While it is tempting to reject Adamski's evidence, the film would be very complex to fake.

THE MEXICAN WAVE

The 1990s has seen an explosion of video evidence, thanks largely to incredible events

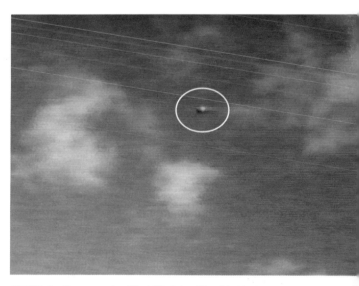

ABOVE: *Another example of the UFOs being filmed in Mexico. This image, filmed in Puebla, southeast of the capital, was filmed by at least six other witnesses during the solar eclipse of July 1991.*

The Roswell case

THE INFAMOUS VIDEO FOOTAGE SHOWING THE AUTOPSY OF ALIENS RECOVERED FROM A 1947 CRASH AT ROSWELL IS NOW A CLASSIC. THE CONTENT STILL CANNOT BE TOTALLY DEBUNKED, AND WE CAN LEARN A LOT BY TAKING A CLOSER LOOK ...

Most people know the story. In 1995, British film producer Ray Santilli announced the arrival on the UFO scene of a new piece of footage, showing what he was told was the autopsy of a genuine extraterrestrial entity. The creature had supposedly been recovered from the wreckage of a craft in the New Mexico desert (for all intents and purposes, the Roswell crash, although the dates are inconsistent with other Roswell accounts) and autopsied in front of an army cinematographer.

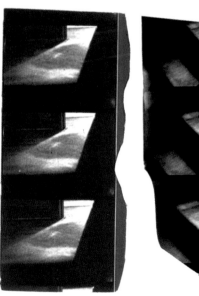

ABOVE: *These strips of film, supposedly from the original autopsy film, were sent for analysis. But where's the alien?*

UNDER ATTACK

The video has come under a lot of due attack from ufologists, surgeons, film-makers and military personnel; and there are certainly gaping holes in the case. A few years of dogged research have revealed that the footage is probably faked —the camera operator was later supposedly involved in filming the departed Elvis—although the attention to detail, production values, and lack of errors and inconsistencies prevent anyone from successfully debunking the content of the footage. We can also learn much from it in other ways. A brief resumé of the multidiscipline research that has gone into its investigation serves as a guide to the kinds of details you should look for when assessing video evidence— and as a warning to hoaxers.

PERIOD DETAIL Check that all the objects in the background date from when the footage was supposedly filmed.

CHEMICAL ANALYSIS Santilli released only a few frames of footage—none of these showed the alien and could have come from any role of exposed film—so little of the stock can be date-verified. If the original film is available,

ABOVE: *The autopsy footage begins with shots of the crash site and a review of the material collected. Among the objects recovered are these panels embossed with six-fingered hands.* BELOW: *A supine alien awaits its rather hasty autopsy. In view are the tools that will be used. These can be assessed for period authenticity. Criticizing the internal organs—or lack of them—is not constructive, as we have no knowledge of alien biology.*

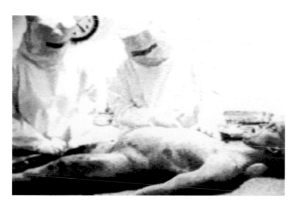

determine when it was manufactured, and exposed, and whether the credible bits come from the same reel as questionable material.

CHRONOLOGY Use background clocks or the positions of clouds or shadows, to authenticate the timescale. The Roswell film takes place over a preposterously short period of time given the fact that an alien lifeform is being autopsied for the first time ever; in reality, it would probably be labored over for hours.

MEDICAL PROCEDURES Pathologists and surgeons have examined the Roswell footage, and most agree that the "surgeons" shown are not fully competent, and that the corpse seems to react in a strange way to surgery (although it is an alien, so who would know?) Try to get specialists to look over any film.

SPECIAL EFFECTS Look for special effects. Many experts feel that the alien in the Roswell film is a very good dummy—based partly on the fact that the shoulders and the fat on the hips do not droop, suggesting the creature is made from an upright body cast.

CHEMICAL ANALYSIS World War II camera operators unanimously agree that the quality of the camera work—more reminiscent of the TV program *NYPD Blue*—is unacceptable. The constant motion and change of focus, and the lack of color (which was used by army operators at the time) suggests a deliberate attempt to blur details.

Drawing conclusions

FROM SNAPSHOTS OF DEAD ALIENS AT CRASH SITES TO VIDEO FOOTAGE OF INTERVIEWS AT AREA 51, IMAGES OF ETS ABOUND. HONE YOUR VISUAL INVESTIGATIVE SKILLS BY TAKING A QUICK TOUR THROUGH SOME MORE CLASSIC EXAMPLES.

In a dimly lit room beneath the Nevada desert, an unusual interview is taking place. Not only is it being conducted in semidarkness in Area 51, the most highly classified science facility in the U.S., but it involves only nonverbal communication. Yet, the hand signals and telepathy being employed are not as bizarre as the subject under interrogation. For this subject, the indistinct creature in the soft glow of a desklamp, is an alien that has been the guest of the American government since crashing its flying saucer on American soil.

This preposterous video is among the latest examples of an alien caught on film. While undoubtedly faked—it has neither the class, budget, scope, nor audacity of its more famous cousin, the autopsy alien—it warns ufologists of the lengths some people will go to confuse them. However, there are other examples of alien images that cannot fairly be ignored. Cases involving such evidence are few and far between, of course. All researchers can do is familiarize themselves with them and extract what information they can.

DNI/27 04:02:58:19

HOWARD MENGER

For the most part, contactees are the most fruitful sources of alien images, thanks largely to their ability to get up close and personal. One such witnesses is Howard Menger, who snapped a Venusian standing in front of his craft. The quality of Menger's Venusian matches his testimony—blurred

LEFT: *The "alien interview" footage was supposedly smuggled out of Area 51 by a disgruntled security guard known as "Victor". His identity is known only to a few people, among them Jeff Broadstreet, the distributor of the footage, who himself acknowledges the likelihood of it being faked.*

ABOVE: *This polaroid image of a Venusian, taken in 1956, is one of the many taken by contactee Howard Menger. The haziness is supposedly "electromagnetic flux'" generated by the craft.*

and indistinct—because, according to Menger, the aliens wanted to infiltrate the human race, and photos could reveal their true identity.

JEFF GREENHAW

Police chief Jeff Greenhaw took four polaroid shots of a six-foot-tall alien in a metallic suit near Falkville, Alabama, on October 17, 1973, after being called to the site by a witness who had reported the landing of a UFO. Within two weeks of taking the photos, Greenhaw's life took a turn for the worse, and he lost his car, home, wife, and job. The arsonist who destroyed his car and house also incinerated the original prints.

With photographic proof of aliens, it is likely to be circumstantial evidence that will point to an explanation. We don't know what aliens look like, so proof cannot be dismissed as "un-alien." Apart from analyzing the image as explained previously, all the investigator can do is thoroughly interrogate the photographer. Photographic cases should be treated exactly the same as normal cases. If witnesses or photographers are not available, all that is left is to research the circumstances surrounding the origin of the image.

LEFT: *The "Falkville Giant," photographed by police chief Jeff Greenhaw in 1973 just before it ran off at great speed, outpacing Greenhaw's patrol car. The original prints were destroyed by an arsonist who burned down Greenhaw's home, suggesting that someone may have been trying to discredit him.*

ABOVE: *This bizarre creature, supposedly fished out of a UFO crash near Mexico City sometime in the 1950s, died shortly afterward. Little else is known about the image, although researchers have theorized that the image is a composite, and that the alien is, in fact, a shaved monkey.*

CHAPTER FIVE

Research

Wonder rather than life is the root of knowledge.
ABRAHAM JOSHUA HESCHEL

Are the governments of the world withholding UFO evidence? According to many ufologists, the answer is yes. They feel that the wealth of declassified material on UFOs—and the volume of material that remains classified—proves that Earth is being visited by extraterrestrial intelligences, and that governments are only too well aware of this.

A CASE OF INCOMPETENCE

To skeptics, the same data paints a completely different picture. They claim that, while there is no doubt that governments have collected UFO information, there is no evidence that any of it is being withheld because it supports the extraterrestrial hypothesis. And anyway, they suggest, the incompetence of governments makes it impossible for secrets to be kept for any length of time. However, one thing is certain whatever your views are—there is a great deal to be learned about UFOs by undertaking research in this area, delving into library resources and national archives. The findings of the major official UFO studies—particularly Blue Book and the Condon Report—are as relevant today as they were when they were first published, and are required reading for anyone who really wants to understand about UFOs and their history.

MAIN PICTURE: *For many, the White House symbolizes the freedom and opportunity at the heart of the American people and presidency; to some ufologists, however, it is an ivory tower in which the secrets of the government's liaison with aliens are hidden. There is even the theory that extraterrestrials have at one time lived—or still live—on Pennsylvania Avenue.*

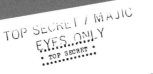

TOP SECRET / MAJIC
EYES ONLY
• TOP SECRET •

00?

• TOP SECRET •

COPY ONE OF ONE.

EYES ONLY

SUBJECT: OPERATION MAJESTIC-12 PRELIMINARY BRIEFING FOR
PRESIDENT-ELECT EISENHOWER.

DOCUMENT PREPARED 18 NOVEMBER, 1952.

BRIEFING OFFICER: ADM. ROSCOE H. HILLENKOETTER (MJ-1)

NOTE: This document has been prepared as a preliminary briefing
only. It should be regarded as introductory to a full operations
briefing intended to follow.

• • • • • •

OPERATION MAJESTIC-12 is a TOP SECRET Research and Development/
Intelligence operation responsible directly and only to th~
President of the United States. Operations of the projec
carried out under control of the Majestic-12 (Majic-12) (
which was established by special classified executive or
President Truman on 24 September, 1947, upon recommenda
Dr. Vannevar Bush and Secretary James Forrestal. (See
"A".) Members of the Majestic-12 Group were designate

Adm. Roscoe H. Hillenkoetter
Dr. Vannevar Bush
Secy. James V. Forrestal*
Gen. Nathan F. Twining
Gen. Hoyt S. Vandenberg
Dr. Detlev Bronk
Dr. Jerome Hunsaker
Mr. Sidney W. Souers
Mr. Gordon Gray
Dr. Donald Menzel
Gen. Robert M. Montague
Dr. Lloyd V. Berkner

The death of Secretary Forrestal on 22 May,
a vacancy which remained unfilled until 01
which date Gen. Walter B. Smith was designat
replacement.

TOP SECRET

TOP SECRET / MAJ!
EYES ONLY
EYES ONLY

The Majestic-12 documents encapsulate the grand-unified UFO cover-up theory: alien technology is recovered in a saucer crash in Roswell, New Mexico, in 1947, and an above-top-secret team of government and military scientists keep the story from the public. The question is: are the documents genuine? The debate continues ...

ABOVE: *The intelligence community in Britain is symbolized by MI6, the agency made famous in the James Bond stories. Along with sister agency MI5 and the Ministry of Defence, this clandestine department is undoubtedly interested in the invasion of British airspace by unidentified "foreign" objects.*
LEFT: *The FBI—the supposed home of the real X-Files—also has a proven interest in UFOs and aliens.*

DEPARTMENT OF JUSTICE
FEDERAL BUREAU OF INVESTIGATION
FIDELITY BRAVERY INTEGRITY

Of no defense significance?

ACCORDING TO DOCUMENTATION RELEASED BY VARIOUS GOVERNMENTS, UFOS ARE "OF NO DEFENSE SIGNIFICANCE." BUT MIGHT THEY BE HIDING SOMETHING? HOW FAR OFF IS A REAL-LIFE *WAR OF THE WORLDS*?

On March 25, 1998, Peter Gersten, the attorney acting on behalf of the UFO group Citizens Against UFO Secrecy (CAUS), filed a lawsuit against the US Department of the Army. The previous September, CAUS had requested the release of information relating to the Roswell crash and the fantastical confessions of US Colonel Philip J. Corso (Ret.), and had been informed that no records were available.

After an appeal was rejected, CAUS exercised their right to file a lawsuit. In it, they demanded to see "any and all field reports, scientific analysis reports, medical autopsy reports, photographs and sketches of, and resulting from, the crash of an extraterrestrial vehicle in Roswell, New Mexico, in July 1947."

EARTH-SHATTERING REVELATIONS

The reason for their insistence in the face of such denials is the earth-shattering book *The Day After Roswell* (1991), written by Corso. In 1961, Corso was Chief of the US Army's Foreign Technology Division—although when he accepted the job, little did he know just how "foreign" the technology would be.

In his memoirs, Corso claimed that this technology was, in fact, alien artifacts recovered from an ET vehicle that had crashed in the New Mexico desert in July 1947. He claims that not only was he tasked with covertly disseminating aspects of alien technology to the private sector, but he also learned of a worldwide defense program against the aliens, using technology harnessed from one of their own ships—leading to the "Star Wars Defense Initiative" (SDI).

Corso's confessions stunned the UFO community, who on the whole accept his story. The US Army, of course, denies everything.

ABOVE: *UFO lawyer Peter Gersten has campaigned tirelessly for the release of official government and military documentation regarding the UFO situation in the U.S.*

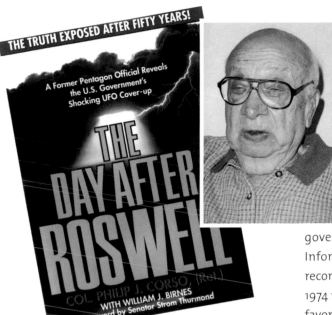

THE TRUTH EXPOSED AFTER FIFTY YEARS!

A Former Pentagon Official Reveals the U.S. Government's Shocking UFO Cover-up

THE DAY AFTER ROSWELL

COL. PHILIP J. CORSO, (Ret.)
WITH WILLIAM J. BIRNES
Foreword by Senator Strom Thurmond

ABOVE: *"We knew who the real targets of SDI were,"* claimed Colonel Philip J. Corso, author of The Day After Roswell, *"and it wasn't a bunch of warheads. It was the UFOs: alien spaceships thinking themselves invulnerable as they soared around the edges of our atmosphere."*

WHAT CAN YOU DO?

If the "official" line is that the discussion is more or less closed, how do you go about researching government and military involvement in the UFO phenomenon? Since 1947—saucerology's "year zero"—the American government has been involved in the collection and analysis of UFO data, and this material can be accessed in numerous ways.

OFFICIAL STUDIES Twinkle, Sign, Grudge, Blue Book, Stork, and Fang are all codenames applied to official U.S. government UFO research between

1947 and 1969. During this time, 12,618 sightings were reported in the U.S., 701 of them remaining unidentified. One report concluded that 30 percent of their cases resisted explanation. So, if up to 30 percent of cases are "unknown," how can officials dismiss them as a non-risk so brusquely?

FREEDOM OF INFORMATION ACT In 1966, Congress heralded a new era of government openness with the Freedom of Information Act, allowing public access to records and policy statements. Amendments in 1974 widened the scope of the Act in the public's favor. This Act was also put in place in Australia, but not in Britain, and eventually saw the release of the first UFO document, in February 1978. It continues to assist ufologists in their search for the truth.

DEEP THROATS If there is a cosmic Watergate-style cover-up, then where are the "Deep Throats" (the name of the secret source who leaked information during the Watergate affair)? Quite a few UFO whistle-blowers have surfaced, although the veracity of their claims is dubious. Most government, military, or agency Deep Throats will approach a researcher with information, although some leading ufologists have their own informants (or at least give the impression that they do). The danger of being approached by someone "on the inside," or of receiving alleged classified documentation, is that it could well be disinformation, spread to discredit either individual researchers or the field of ufology generally.

The official story

OFFICIAL U.S. GOVERNMENT REPORTS ON UFOS MAY HAVE LEFT MANY DISSATISFIED, BUT THEY TELL US MUCH ABOUT GOVERNMENTAL ATTITUDES TO THE SUBJECT.

Lieutenant General Nathan Twining convinced Army Air Force Headquarters to undertake Project Sign—the first of the highly classified investigations of UFOs—with the following words: "The phenomenon reported is something real and not visionary or fictitious."

PROJECT SIGN Sign was initiated on January 22, 1948, and investigators theorized that Thomas Mantell died while chasing the planet Venus, demonstrating their inexperience in UFO research.

Sign officers divided into three camps: those who strove to explain all cases in terms of natural phenomena; those who believed that secret craft had breached Churchill's recently raised Iron Curtain; and those who supported the ETH, including project leader, Robert Sneider. The Pentagon disagreed with the last group and had all copies of their *Estimate of the Situation* burned.

PROJECT GRUDGE On December 16, 1948, Sign was dissolved. The UFO program remained, but under the more telling name of Grudge. Ufology entered the Dark Ages: pro-ET Sign staff were replaced, and the "of no defense significance" view prevailed once more. Then, suddenly, the Army Signals Corp at Fort Monmouth, New Jersey, picked up a UFO on radar. Grudge was underway again.

RIGHT: *Two of the personnel of the official American investigations codenamed Sign and Grudge: Captain Edward J Ruppelt (standing) and Major General John Samford.*

PROJECT BLUE BOOK A new director, Captain Edward J. Ruppelt, was appointed. He completely revitalized Grudge, and the project merged with an Ohio-based study of Soviet military technology called Project Stork. Within six months of Ruppelt's arrival, the UFO investigators received an official title—Aerial Phenomena Group—and a new codename: Blue Book (Blue was the Army codeword for "sky"). The golden age of ufology had arrived.

In 1952, a fleet of UFOs appeared on radar over Washington, some of them allegedly buzzing the

ABOVE: *Hector J. Quintanilla and the staff of the USAF's Project Blue Book. Quintanilla became known as "Master of the Possible," as he concluded that most UFOs were "possible" birds or aircraft.*

WORLDWIDE RESEARCH

The U.S. is not the only country to conduct official UFO studies. In Britain, UFO data before 1962 has supposedly been incinerated, but files available at the Public Records Office are worth accessing. During the 1950s, George Ward, Secretary of State for Air, commented: "Until I've got a saucer ... in Hyde Park and can charge the public sixpence a go to enter, [UFOs] must be balloons, otherwise the government would fall and I'd lose my job." Today, officials who have gone public with their doubts still say that there is no cover-up.

AUSTRALIAN RESEARCH *In Australia and New Zealand, research falls under the jurisdiction of the Royal Australian Air Force. Studies have concluded that most cases can be explained, although officials refuse to publish exact data.*

White House. Reeling from such a breach of restricted airspace, the Central Intelligence Agency (CIA) convened a panel of scientists to assess official UFO data to date. The panel cast a skeptical eye over the Blue Book reports, and, partly as a result of this, Blue Book went the way of Grudge.

UFOs were back in the Dark Ages. Investigations became cursory, and Ruppelt published his *The Report on Unidentified Flying Objects* (1956), confirming many people's suspicions that the government was trying to cover up information.

CONDON COMMITTEE Throughout the 1960s, under Major Hector J. Quintanilla, Blue Book continued to deteriorate. Attempts were made to establish a civilian group, to prevent the project from becoming an Air force puppet. "Impartiality" was offered by the University of Colorado, and prominent nuclear physicist Edward U. Condon accepted the task of heading a two-year study.

Unfortunately, little was gained by the University of Colorado's investigation. Condon felt that the scientific study of UFOs was "pointless," and a cynical tone ran through his committee's research and its concluding report, *Scientific Study of Unidentified Flying Objects* (1968). Although Condon's opinion was refuted by the American Institute of Astronautics and Aeronautics, Blue Book was closed within a year of publication.

RIGHT: *Dr. Edward Uhler Condon led the University of Colorado's UFO study. He concluded that UFOs were not worthy of scientific study.*

Independent research

THE UNIVERSAL FASCINATION WITH UFOS HAS STIMULATED A NUMBER OF INDEPENDENT SURVEYS. THESE RESEARCHERS ARE FREE TO EXPRESS THEIR OPINIONS ... BUT COULD THEY BE OVERLY BIASED **TOWARD** THE ETH?

The following list runs through selected highlights from the history of independent UFO research. Such studies usually take one of two forms: quantitative research into sightings and experiences, or collating case studies to support a given point of view. Most of the resulting reports are available from the larger UFO groups and, despite their often strong ET bias, make fascinating reading.

ABOVE: *In 1958, during a live TV interview, US Marine Corp Major Donald Keyhoe was taken off air—for "national security" reasons —while discussing his belief that aliens were visiting Earth.*

NICAP One of the earliest and most influential UFO groups, the National Investigations Committee on Aerial Phenomena (NICAP), actively sought to expose what they saw as a UFO cover-up and pushed for congressional hearings. In addition to assisting in data collection for the University of Colorado UFO Project, NICAP released one of the first UFO magazines, *The UFO Investigator*.

JAMES MCDONALD Arguably the most important individual researcher was James E. McDonald, an atmospheric physicist from the University of Arizona. Following a UFO sighting in 1954, and after failed attempts to establish or join a UFO study independent of Blue Book, McDonald took it upon himself to investigate UFOs. His major contribution was in re-investigating Blue Book cases, using his expert knowledge to debunk the debunking. His own study was presented to Congress's House Committee on Science and Astronautics in 1968, in which he concludes that 41 cases were "unknowns."

ROPER SURVEY The Roper Organization carried out a survey designed by ufologists Budd Hopkins and David Jacobs to study "Unusual Personal Experiences." It was this poll, of around 6,000 people, that concluded that one in fifty Americans are "probably" abductees. The study has come under fire from many angles, not least because indicators used to signify an "abduction" matched those for sleep paralysis and associated hallucinations (*see pages* 74–75).

GALLUP SURVEYS

To the right is the percentage of Americans who answered "yes" to questions posed by the Gallup Organization since 1978. The value of such reports are limited, as it does not account for the "don't knows," and the definition of UFO may not be fully understood—it is likely to mean "intelligently controlled extraterrestrial flying saucer."

QUESTION	1996	1990	1978
Have you heard or read about UFOs?	87	90	93
Have you seen a UFO?	12	14	9
Are UFOs real?	48	47	57
Have UFOs visited Earth in some form?	45	–	–
Is there life elsewhere in the universe?	72	–	–
Is there humanlike life elsewhere in the universe?	38	46	15

The belief in UFOs outweighs belief in ghosts and astrology, but is outnumbered by belief in the Devil (56%) and angels (72%).

BEST AVAILABLE EVIDENCE During the 1990s, venture-capitalist Laurance Rockefeller provided financial support to a select band of ufologists. His goal, realized in 1997, was the report *Unidentified Flying Objects: The Best Available Evidence*. A true Fortean and eclectic, Rockefeller appears to have no opinion on the subject and allegedly donated $30,000 toward the 169-page report in order to present the findings to world leaders.

STURROCK REPORT In 1998, a panel of scientists announced their opinions on UFO data presented by eight ufologists. Organized by Peter Sturrock, professor of Applied Physics at Stanford University, and supported by the Society of Scientific Exploration, the review covered "information about unusual phenomena currently unknown to science." Sturrock's review concluded by supporting ongoing UFO research, but rejected the ETH.

ABOVE AND LEFT:
Ufologists and abductee counselors Budd Hopkins and David Jacobs designed the Roper survey, a questionnaire completed by more than 6,000 people, which concluded that one in fifty Americans are "probably" abductees.

Freedom of information

DECLASSIFIED AND CENSORED DOCUMENTS RELEASED BY GOVERNMENT AGENCIES CAN PROVIDE THE "SMOKING GUN" THAT UFOLOGISTS NEED TO ARGUE THEIR CASE.

In the USA, about eighty percent of the population believe that their government is withholding evidence of UFOs. Whether or not this is actually the case, an ordinance known as the Freedom of Information Act (FOIA) became law in 1974, allowing ordinary citizens to access official government, military or federal records. Since the enactment of the FOIA, thousands of pages of declassified documents relating in some way to UFOs have been released.

LEGAL OBLIGATIONS

The act entitles anyone from any country to submit a request in writing regarding any subject they wish, and the targeted agency is legally obliged to provide the information. Many UFO groups, such as Citizens Against UFO Secrecy (CAUS), have targeted their efforts on forcing the release of documents through the FOIA. There are stumbling blocks to overcome in the fight for access, such as official exemption clauses dealing with foreign policy, invasion of privacy and so on, and the possible cost of gaining information that officials feel is not of "genuine public interest." However, your chances will be greatly improved by making the right kind of application letter, and the pointers included on this page might well apply broadly to any letter written to an official body in pursuit of sensitive material.

Once you have dispatched your request, you should receive confirmation of receipt. If the request cannot be fulfilled for some reason, you should be told why and what you can do about it. It can take months or years to receive information. Once a request has been accepted, contact the appropriate office every four to six weeks. There are four main outcomes to your request:

REQUEST GRANTED In rare cases, you will be delivered exactly what you asked for, without exclusions or censorship. If there are any missing pages, or gaps in the serial numbers of documents, you may appeal for more data to be released.

REQUEST DENIED IN PART You may receive only a selected portion of the requested documentation. Again, you can appeal. Ask for a listing of omissions along with justification for each denial.

REQUEST DENIED IN FULL As with partial denials, you can make an administrative appeal. If all else fails, you can file a lawsuit to enforce the release of censured portions.

NO RECORDS If the agency believes that no file exists, check your original letter for ways in which the phrasing might be misleading. If you have reason to believe that the agency has information, make an appeal stating why.

ADDRESS: *If it's an FOIA matter, mark your envelope "Attention: FOIA Request," and mail it to the appropriate FOIA office. If dealing with the FBI, send one copy to the headquarters in Washington DC and one to the field office(s) nearest to the location of the event mentioned in your request.*

SUBJECT: *State the subject you are researching. Provide as much detail as you can (dates, locations, names of alleged witnesses etc.) and use official/formal terms such as anomalous aerial activity where possible; requests for "UFOs" will merely result in a standard response regarding that agency's stance on the matter.*

DENIALS: *To assist in the appeals process, ask for an inventory of all denied information, with reasons for the denials. If you feel you can refute these reasons, you may be more successful in your appeal. Also, ask for the level of classification involved, as this may reveal some clues, or help you refute the reasons for denial.*

CENSORING *Insist that any censoring is done in black, in order that you can identify the extent of the denial.*

APPEALS *To warn officers that you might appeal, and to save time, ensure that you ask for the address and contact name to whom you can address an appeal.*

FEES *Always state your belief that the request is in the public's interest. You may be asked to demonstrate that the data is of national interest, which should not be difficult.*

GENERAL APPROACH: *A badly written or insubstantial letter may not secure you the information you desire, while a detailed and comprehensive one will save you a lot of time in the long run and may provide you with what you want first time around. Don't forget to make a photocopy of the letter before you send it out and put it in a regularly updated file of all related correspondence and phone calls. Once sent, continue to press the relevant agency for an update.*

FOIA Unit
FOIA Agency Address

Your name
Your address
Your telephone number
Date

Request under the Freedom of Information Act.

This is a request for a complete search of all filing systems and locations for all records held by your agency relating to:

insert details of the desired records, or describe in detail the event(s) for which you seek information,

including all documentation, including captions, that includes reference to:

insert possible alternative names and spellings, abbreviations, acronyms, etc.

I also request all "see references" to these names.

If the documents are denied in part or whole, please specify which exemptions are claimed for each passage or whole document denied. Please provide a complete itemized inventory and detailed factual justification of any denial. Specify the number of pages in each document and the total number of pages pertaining to this request. For classified material denied, please include the following information:

- the classification rating (confidential, secret, top secret, etc.)
- the identity of the classifier
- the date or event for automatic declassification or classification review

I request that censored material be 'blacked out' rather than 'whited out' or cut out. I expect that the remaining non-exempt portions of documents will be released.

Please send a memo to the appropriate units in your office or agency to assure that no records related to this request are destroyed (and please send a copy of the memo to me). Please advise of any destruction of records, and include the date and authority for such destruction.

As I expect to appeal against any denials, please specify the office and address to which an appeal should be directed.

I believe that my request qualifies for a waiver of fees as the release of the information would benefit the general public and be in the public interest.

I can be reached at the telephone number listed above. Please call rather than write if there are any questions or if you need additional information from me.

I expect a response to this request within ten working days, as provided for in the Freedom of Information Act.

Sincerely, etc

ABOVE: *An example of a letter that can be written to receive documentation from any Freedom of Information Act office.*

Deep throats

THE "DEEP THROATS" WHO RISK ALL TO LEAK INFORMATION ABOUT UFOS AND THE AUTHORITIES MAY BE A VALUABLE SOURCE OF CLASSIFIED INFORMATION, BUT HOW FAR CAN THEY BE TRUSTED?

To fans of *The X Files*, the character of the UFO "mole" Deep Throat will be well known. Originally, this was the pseudonym of the Executive Branch source who leaked information to the *Washington Post* during the Watergate affair and comes from the title of a celebrated porn movie—a bastardization of the journalistic jargon "deep background."

The main problem with Deep Throats in the world of ufology—usually government, military, or intelligence insiders who make the first move

and approach ufologists—is never knowing their agenda. There are two principal motives:

- *To let the public know the "truth" about our contact with aliens*
- *To spread disinformation in order to throw ufologists off the scent.*

In the first instance, there is no guarantee that it is the truth that is being leaked, so the ufologist must be very wary. The history of UFO Deep Throats is dark and sordid. The best policy is to accept any information and then verify it later, a task that can take years of frustrating research.

THE AVIARY "We are continuing the investigation of UFO sightings and landings in an official capacity, sanctioned by the government, but clandestinely." So claimed an anonymous intelligence Deep Throat known only as Falcon, on the television program *UFO Cover-up? ... Live*.

Falcon, and co-conspirator Condor, claimed that military intelligence had made contact with aliens after the crash at Roswell, that the aliens were visiting from the Zeta Reticuli star system, and that they liked Tibetan music and strawberry ice cream.

Condor and Falcon came to prominence, thanks to William Moore, a former Special Agent in the Air Force Office of Special Investigations. In 1980, while

ABOVE: William Moore is one of the many ufologists to become involved with the clandestine group known as the Aviary.

MICHAEL WOLF Strange goings-on at Area 51 were "confirmed" by computer scientist "Dr." Michael Wolf, self-professed Chancellor Emeritus of the New England Institute for Advanced Research, in his book, *Catchers of Heavens*. His credentials and claims have also been completely denounced.

COOPER & ENGLISH At the close of Project Blue Book, a total of 13 reports had been published, although the last was numbered 14. The exclusion of number 13 is usually put down to tristaidekaphobia—fear of the number 13—although, in the late 1980s, a new theory emerged. It was said that report 13 had been suppressed because it contained sensitive information. The source of these claims were Milton William Cooper, a former petty officer in the Pacific fleet, and William English, a former American soldier stationed in Britain, both of whom reported reading the missing report.

The details recounted by Cooper and English are undoubtedly false, but the documents may be real. It is not unknown for military leaders to test the reliability of subordinates by feeding them fantastical information and monitoring the result —English was fired after making his revelations ...

promoting his book *The Roswell Incident*, Moore was approached by a man who claimed to work at the Kirtland Air Force Base. Falcon became the contact between Moore and a group of intelligence officers, all of whom took bird names as pseudonyms: now collectively known as The Aviary.

Moore began trading services for inside information. One of his more nefarious activities was monitoring the pursuits of ufologist Paul Bennewitz. Acting as an intermediary between Bennewitz and The Aviary, Moore passed on disinformation to Bennewitz who, deluged with lies, became overwhelmed with paranoia and suffered a nervous breakdown in 1985.

BOB LAZAR Another Deep Throat whistling like a canary about the whole Roswell story is Robert Lazar, a physicist who claimed to have worked on a recovered flying saucer at S4, a facility within Area 51. Lazar is the principal source of information on the ET projects in this top-secret base, but his background is dubious and his qualifications are possibly false. However, many ufologists choose to overlook this in favor of his compelling claims.

RIGHT: Robert "Bob" Lazar claimed to have worked on recovered alien technology at Area 51. However, he has a dubious background and education—although Lazar claims that this was why he was given the job: so that he could be discredited easily.

The mystery of the MJ-12 documents

ONE OF THE MOST INTERESTING LEAKED DOCUMENT CASES IS THE INFAMOUS MJ-12 AFFAIR—MAJESTIC-12 BEING THE GOVERNMENT TEAM SAID TO HAVE BEEN CREATED TO INVESTIGATE AND COVER UP THE REAL FINDINGS AT ROSWELL.

In December 1984, in the middle of on-going UFO research, TV producer Jaime Shandera received a roll of undeveloped 35-mm film through the mail. Developing the film revealed a classified briefing paper dated November 18, 1952, and addressed to president-elect Dwight D. Eisenhower. The National Security information at the head of the page reads "TOP SECRET/MAJIC EYES ONLY" and a warning at the foot announces that "the material herein is strictly limited to those possessing Majestic-12 clearance level." The reason for the secrecy? Clearly typewritten on the third page is the revelation that a "local rancher reported that one [disk-shaped flying object] had crashed in a remote region of New Mexico located approximately seventy-five miles northwest of Roswell Army Air Field."

ABOVE: Jaime Shandera, recipient of the MJ-12 papers. His close involvement in the story has led some researchers to conclude that he may have faked the documents himself.

"COVERT ANALYTICAL EFFORT"

The author of the briefing paper, Admiral Roscoe H. Hillenkoetter (aka "MJ-1"), went on to explain to the newly-elected Eisenhower that "four small humanlike beings" had ejected from the craft before impact and that their dead bodies, and their craft, had been recovered for scientific study. "A covert analytical effort" had been organized by Majestic-12, a team of government scientists and military and intelligence officers, their remit being to "determine the method of propulsion or the nature or method of transmission of the power source involved."

Finally, the document ends with an appendix (the first, and only, of eight supposedly attached to the original briefing sheet). This single page, on White House paper stamped with TOP SECRET EYES ONLY, is a letter dated September 24, 1947 from President Harry Truman, authorizing his Secretary of Defense, James V. Forrestal, to establish "Operation Majestic Twelve." So, does this prove conclusively that the Roswell crash really was an extraterrestrial incident, and that there is indeed a "Cosmic Watergate" underway?

CONTINUING CONTROVERSY

The debate as to the authenticity of the MJ-12 papers still rages 15 years after the documents first surfaced. Other, equally controversial MJ-12 documents have since come to light, but they have done little to settle the debate. The very nature of the MJ-12 documents sparks controversy

—anonymous postings, undeveloped film, highly classified government documents—and their story reads like a spy thriller. So, too, does the effort to authenticate the papers. At the forefront of research is Roswell researcher Stanton Friedman who, after a grueling eleven-year study, is convinced of the document's authenticity. His incredibly detailed book, *TOP SECRET/MAJIC*, faced a barrage of criticism on publication in 1996, yet Friedman has confronted even his fiercest critics.

BELOW AND RIGHT: Did the Majestic-12 documents ever grace the desk of presidents Truman and Eisenhower (right)? If so, the so-called "Cosmic Watergate" has been confirmed; if not, it would suggest a disinformation campaign. But by whom? And why?

Authenticating documents

AUTHENTICATING QUESTIONABLE DOCUMENTATION IS A HIGHLY SKILLED TASK,
BUT THERE ARE CERTAIN CLEAR GUIDELINES TO HELP THOSE BRAVE ENOUGH
TO ATTEMPT IT.

There are two main aspects to analyzing a document. One is the need to establish the truth or otherwise of the material—an arduous task that may take years of library, archive, and face-to-face research. Every fact and date must be verified or rejected, every signature authenticated, and every personality researched. The model for such tasks is Friedman's book, *TOP SECRET/MAJIC*.

Of higher priority, however, is the authentication of the documents themselves. Before undertaking any research, it is vital that the papers, microfilms, films, envelopes, and stamps are validated by a qualified document analyst. This should identify forgeries and hoaxes simply from the documents' corporeality (examination of the papers, ink, watermarks, and so on) and to a lesser extent incorporeality (handwriting, style of language, etc.)

Generally, documents available at archives will be legitimate and not require authentication. If you receive paperwork anonymously, however, desk and forensic research will be needed. On these pages are annotated images from the MJ-12 film to help you assess questionable documents.

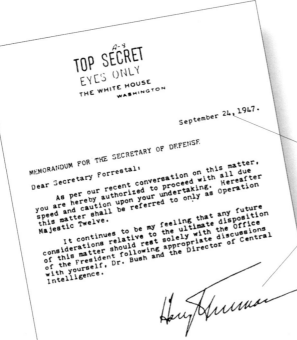

DATE FORMAT *Look for consistency of style—for example, month/day/year or day/month/year—in consecutive documentation. If the author uses one system, then suddenly switches, expect a forgery.*

SIGNATURES *No two consecutive signatures are the same, and replica signatures are rare to the point of improbable. Fakes may be: unresearched, with no attempt at forgery; simulated freehand; traced; or genuine, but obtained by deception. Obtain copies of authenticated signatures and use a magnifying glass to look for shaky lines, poor quality loops, etc. Examine around the signature for cut-and-paste marks.*

DATA ACCURACY *Check that the document could have been produced on the day claimed. Cross-refer dates in the document with the schedules of the author and any personalities mentioned. Confirm that any action mentioned, such as meetings or briefings, actually took place on the day(s) in question. If the author was on vacation, for example, he is unlikely to have been able to sign anything.*

TYPEWRITER MODEL *Check that the same typewriter was used for documents prepared in the same office. Compare typewriter styles on documents prepared at the same period (available from national archives) as the document in question. With older typewriters, it is often possible to identify the model used by the characters. With modern electric typewriters or word processors, this task becomes more difficult, but not impossible. Look for use of a corrections ribbon to assess any obliterations or over-typing.*

INDENTED WRITING *Expert analysis may search for any hand- or typewriting from sheets of paper that might have been placed on top of the questioned sheet. The pressure of the writing may go through to sheets below, and an instrument known as an Electrostatic Detection Apparatus can reveal this. A more low-tech option is to shine a light on the document and alter the angle of the beam until indentations can be seen.*

REFERENCES *Check for any consecutive numbering. So, if a document has a reference number of 245, make sure that there is not already a genuine 245, and that there is a 244 and 246 from the same office.*

INK ANALYSIS *Analysis of an ink's chemical composition determines the type and date of production, and is useful for dating older documents. For "younger" inks, up to six months old, the date is established using tests to measure how fast the ink can be chemically removed from the paper.*

PAPER ANALYSIS *If you have access to original papers, the first task is to authenticate the paper stock. Originals cannot be removed from archives, so be suspicious—or suspect disinformation. Is the paper the same as that used around the time the document was written? Is there a watermark? If so, can you contact the manufacturer for confirmation that a federal agency bought the paper?*

PSYCHOLINGUISTIC ANALYSIS *By examining individual and collective use of words, hidden or subconscious detail can be revealed and a psychological profile of the author built up. Is the tone of a letter appropriate for the office from which it originates? Is slang used, suggesting that the document is more contemporary, or written by someone from a different background to the supposed author?*

Calling deep space ... the search for signs of life

IN CALIFORNIA, A BAND OF ENTHUSIASTS IS ATTEMPTING TO MAKE CONTACT WITH EXTRATERRESTRIALS. BUT THEY'RE NOT MEMBERS OF A NEW AGE OR SAUCER CULT—THEY'RE SCIENTISTS HARNESSING THE LATEST SPACE-AGE TECHNOLOGY.

The Search for Extraterrestrial Intelligence (SETI) is a multimillion-dollar research project, funded irregularly by NASA, that uses radio telescopy to scan the heavens for signs of extraterrestrial intelligence. First proposed in 1959 by two scientists at Cornell University, the search for aliens became a reality in 1960 when a 650-foot-wide microwave telescope was aimed at the stars Epsilon Eridani and Tau Cetifor.

The search proved fruitless. However, the Cornell team established the foundations for a scientific—and respected—search for aliens. Since then, millions of dollars have been invested, and millions of radio channels monitored. So far, apart from a few red herrings—for example, when seemingly intelligent signals were finally traced to a microwave oven in the cafeteria next door!—our galactic neighbors have remained silent.

The premise of SETI is simple: any sufficiently evolved civilization will give off some kind of signal, probably in the form of electromagnetic radiation. Like us, they will probably be sending out signals in order to be detected.

INTERGALACTIC HAYSTACK

This is all very well, but do we have the capability to detect any signals? Stabbing in the dark for extraterrestrial life is like trying to find a needle in an infinitely large haystack while blindfolded and with your hands and feet tied. And there may not even be a needle ... SETI scientists, however, are convinced of their task.

There is something of a split between SETIzens —who mostly do not believe in the ETH for the UFO

LEFT: The Parkes radio telescope in New South Wales, Australia, listens for radio signals from other solar systems like ours as part of the Phoenix SETI project.

ABOVE & LEFT: The Arecibo telescope in Puerto Rico sent this binary code into deep space to tell any ET intelligence where and who we are, and that we are DNA-based lifeforms.

SETI@HOME For armchair SETIzens, the University of California at Berkeley offers the chance to use a home computer to analyze raw data from the Arecibo radio telescope. Project SERENDIP (Search for Extraterrestrial Radio Emissions from Nearby Developed Intelligent Populations), on-line from April 1999, taps into the idle resource of PCs in the form of a screensaver that sifts through SETI data while the computer is idle. Simply download the software and data from the Internet and let your computer get to work. Contact seti@home.com

phenomenon—and ufologists, many of whom believe that SETI is pointless since there is enough evidence already. I advocate sitting on the interstellar fence while keeping a foot in each camp—the more evidence the better. With this in mind, here are two suggestions for taking part in the search:

PROJECT ARGUS Named after the all-seeing Greek guard with 100 eyes, Argus is the project of the SETI League, a grassroots, not-for-profit organization based in New Jersey. The League was formed in 1994 after Congress pulled all NASA SETI funding, and today it has about 500 members.

This is probably the most ambitious radio-astronomy project that does not receive official funding. The aim is to use as many radio telescopes as possible to detect emissions. SETI League advocates building your own radio telescope. For more information, see http://www.setileague.org

THE DRAKE EQUATION

T*he SETI Institute's Frank Drake, one of the first astronomers to consider radio telescopy for an alien hunt, has devised a formula that be believes proves the existence of extraterrestrial intelligence:*

$$N = R \times f_p \times n_e \times f_l \times f_i \times f_c \times L$$

The number of intelligent civilizations out there (N), is dependent on: the number of new star formations (R), the percentage of those capable of sustaining life (f_p), the percentage of those that are Earthlike (n_e), and the probability that life will actually form (f_l), become technologically advanced (f_i), and have any desire to contact Earth (f_c). These are all multiplied together and by the estimated life expectancy of such a civilization.

No one really knows what figures to include in this extraordinary and somewhat misguided formula, but Drake has speculated an audacious figure in the tens of millions.

CHAPTER SIX

Hotspots

He who has not traveled does not
know the value of a man.

ARAB PROVERB

Over the last hundred years, since researchers began logging accounts of mysterious aerial activity, UFO incidents have been recorded in waves. These irregular eruptions of reports—known as "UFO flaps"—have been attributed to a variety of factors (*see* box opposite).

UFO LABORATORIES

Whichever theory, if any, is correct, the UFO flap is an undisputed universal phenomenon that continues to manifest itself. Areas of concentrated UFO activity are known as hotspots and can be treated by ufologists as "UFO laboratories," as J. Allen Hynek put it. The globe is littered with areas now synonymous with UFOs—Gulf Breeze, Mexico City, Bonnybridge, Bass Straits, Hessdalen, the Nevada desert—any of which can, and should, be visited by the keen ufologist wanting to get more involved in their hobby. Hotspots offer a fascinating insight into the people and places of ufology, and this chapter gives you some essential background to these areas. You may be interested in organizing or taking part in a skywatch, or getting in touch with key witnesses. Or you might simply want to visit one of these now-legendary places on vacation. The UFO world awaits, so get packing—perhaps you'll experience a strange encounter of your own ...

MAIN PICTURE: *If UFOs won't come to you, perhaps you could go to the UFOs. Visiting a hotspot may not provide a dramatic encounter, but it will add a new dimension to your interest.*

UFO FLAPS: THE KEY THEORIES

In his award-winning essay *UFO Flaps*, Martin Kottmeyer outlines the key theories about waves of UFO reports:

• **ALIEN RECONNAISSANCE** *UFOs are ET craft visiting Earth to monitor nuclear testing. This is the reason that the year 1947 —two years after Hiroshima and Nagasaki —was such a busy year for UFO reports.*

ABOVE AND LEFT: *Artists' impressions of UFOs. In reality, saucers rarely leave themselves so open to photography. If you are going to snap one, however, you could do worse than visit a holspot.*

• **MARTIAN HYPOTHESIS** *There was a general belief that UFO flaps occurred when Mars came closest to Earth. The Red Planet was one of the favored origins for flying saucers, at least until the first probes confirmed the absence of life.*

• **MATHEMATICAL CYCLES** *Certain ufologists interpret statistical UFO data in terms of cyclical patterns. In the first few years of saucerology, for example, UFO flaps occurred in June and July. Supporting this cyclical hypothesis is the Tourist Theory, which states that UFO flaps are ETs vacationing on Earth.*

• **SILLY SEASON** *This theory blames the media for publicizing UFO stories. Ufologists and cynics continue to debate this, often using the same data to support their own positions.*

• **MASS HYSTERIA** *This theory states that waves of public paranoia—inspired by war, political scandal, or movies—produce an increase in UFO reports. Edward Ruppelt, head of Blue Book, stated that a flap was "an advanced degree of confusion that has not yet reached panic proportions."*

Location: *Roswell, New Mexico, USA*

How to get there: *Flights to Albuquerque; take Interstate 40 east, Route 285 south.*

airport
capital
city of interest
city/town
mountains

Event: In July 1947, something crashed in New Mexico, close to Roswell. Roswell Army Air Field (RAAF) personnel recovered the object and initially announced it to be a flying saucer. Officials later withdrew this statement, claiming that it was simply a balloon. The story was forgotten until 1979, when the son of one of the RAAF officers revealed that the material was not of this Earth ...

Being There: Of most interest is the UFO museum. The International UFO Museum and Research Center plays host to a yearly convention on the anniversary of the crash. The Outa Limits UFO Enigma Museum on South Main closed in 1997.

Accommodation
There is no shortage of places to stay in Roswell. The one thing Main Street has more of than papier-mâché aliens is motels, hotels, and guesthouses. In 1997, the 50th anniversary of the crash, a number of hotels were purpose-built for the event.

Useful Contacts
New Mexico Department of Tourism
491 Old Santa Fe Trail
P.O. Box 20003
Santa Fe, NM 87503
Tel: +1-505-827-7400, 1-800-545-2040
Fax: +1-505-827-7402

The International UFO Museum & Research Center
114 N. Main Street
Roswell, NM 88202-6047
Open 7 days a week, 11.00 a.m.–5.00 p.m.
Tel. +1-505-625-9495

Robert H. Goddard Planetarium
Roswell Museum and Art Center
100 West Eleventh Street
Public shows: one week per month at 1.30 p.m.
Tel. +1-505-624-6744

ABOVE: *What crashed in the New Mexico desert at Roswell? A trip to either of the two UFO museums may help you decide. You can also take a bus ride out to one of the alleged crash sites.*

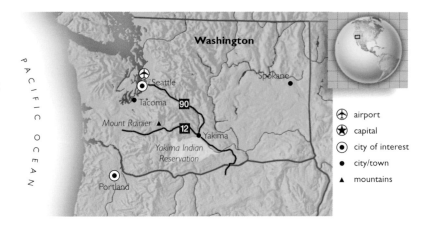

Location: *Mount Rainier, Washington State, USA*

How to get there: *International flights to Seattle; domestic flights to Yakima; drive north to Mount Rainier.*

Event: In 1947, Kenneth Arnold, a 32-year-old businessman and pilot from Boise, Idaho, was flying his single-engine Callair over Mount Rainier in the Cascade Mountains when he observed "a formation of nine bright objects coming from the vicinity of Mount Baker. They were flying very close to the mountaintops and at a tremendous speed. They flew like no aircraft; in fact, they reminded me of a saucer skipping across water."

Being There: On the anniversary of the event, ufologists make the trek to Rainier to commemorate the birth of saucerology. Also of interest is the Yakima Indian Reservation, a well-known site for earthlights. A few hours' drive takes you to Tacoma, where Kenneth Arnold investigated the infamous "Maury Island" incident, in which a dog was killed and a boy injured by debris discharged by one of six UFOs.

Accommodation
Choices of hostels and B&Bs.

Useful Contacts
Washington State Bed and Breakfast guide
Tel: +1-800-647-2918
(24-hr hot-line)

Yakima Valley Visitors & Convention Bureau
10 North 8th Street
Yakima, WA 98901-2521
Tel. +1-800-221-0751

San Juan Islands Visitor Information Service
P.O. Box 65
Lopez Island, WA 98261
Tel. +1-360-468-3663

Spokane Convention & Visitors Bureau
West 926 Sparague Ave., Suite 180
Spokane, WA 99204-0552
Tel. +1-501-624-1341

ABOVE: *It was while flying over Mount Rainier, in the stunning Cascade Mountain range, that pilot Kenneth Arnold had his legendary flying-saucer sighting.*

Location:
Gulf Breeze,
southwestern Florida, USA

How to get there:
International flights into
Miami; Pensacola regional
airport has domestic
flights daily.

Event: On November 11, 1987, a building contractor by the name of Ed Walters witnessed a glowing, blue-gray craft outside his home. He rushed inside to grab his Polaroid, but no sooner had he taken the photo, than a blue beam of light struck him, paralyzing him for a moment. When the paralysis lifted, the object was gone. But Walters had the photographic evidence. From then on, Walters—and many of the locals—have continued to photograph UFOs.

Being there: Beware. Gulf Breeze can be something of a nest of vipers. With over ten years of living in a hotspot, many locals are now actively defrauding ufologists. This is a pity, because some people seem to be having genuine experiences. More usefully, there is also an annual UFO conference and regular sky-watches.

Accommodation
Numerous condominiums and cottages are available for rent, and there are hotels for all budgets. Some researchers find accommodation with locals, but, as said, be careful of who you trust.

Useful Contacts
Gulf Breeze Properties [Accommodation bureau]
41 Via De Luna Drive
Pensacola Beach, Florida 32561
Tel. +1-850-932-3539

Gulf Coast Accommodation
22 Via De Luna Drive
Pensacola Beach, Florida 32561
Tel. +1-850-932-9788

Project Awareness [A field study project organized by the Mutual UFO Network—the world's largest UFO group]
P.O. Box 730
Gulf Breeze, Florida 32562
Tel. +1-904-432-8888 Fax: +1-505-827-7402

ABOVE: *One of the many UFO photographs taken by Ed Walters at Gulf Breeze, Florida. Photographs continue to be taken, so don't forget to take your camera—you never know your luck.*

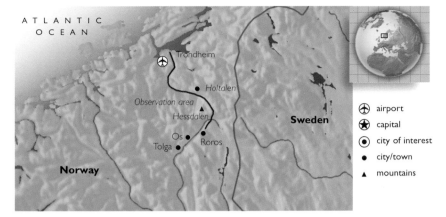

Location: *Hessdalen Valley, Holtaten, Norway*

How to get there: *International flights to Roror; regular bus trips from Roros, Tolga, and other neighboring towns.*

Event: The valley is best known for its strange balls of light, which started to appear in 1981. Up until 1984, they were seen almost daily, with about 15–20 sightings a week, decreasing to about 20 a year. In 1996, there were 17 reports.

Being there: "UFO safari" tours run out of nearby Roros, taking you to all the main spots around Hessdalen, but be sure to book well in advance, as people come from all over the world to see the lights. If you get involved in a night-time sky-watch, or camp for the night, be sure to wrap up warmly, as temperatures can drop well below zero.

ABOVE: *An example of an earthlight as seen in Hessdalen Valley, Norway. Sightings of these plasma balls are becoming more rare at Hessdalen, so be prepared to see nothing if you visit.*

Accommodation

There are four towns in the region of Hessdalen: Roros, Tolga, Os, and Holtalen. All have accommodation readily available, and many UFOlogists choose to live with local families. The brave can camp in the valley, but be warned: the temperature can drop well below zero, so pack warm clothing and hiking boots.

Useful Contacts

UFO Safari Tours
Tel. +47-7241-6173

Roros Accommodation
Bergstadens Hotel
Osloveien 22
Roros
Tel. +47-7240-6080

Quality Roros Hotel
An Margittsvei 7460
Roros
Tel. +47-7241-1011

Haaneset Camping
7460
Roros
Tel. +47-7241 0600
Fax. +47-7241 0601

Tolga Accommodation
Hotel Malmplassen
Gjestegard 2540
Tolga
Tel. +47-6249-4505

Kvennan Camping
2450
Tolga
Tel. +47-6249 4039

Hessdalen Tourist
Information
Tel. +47-6680-3001

Location: *El Yunque region, Puerto Rico*

How to get there: *International flights to Munoz Marin Airport; flights to Ponce, then Route 51 to El Yunque.*

ATLANTIC OCEAN

San Juan
Canovanas
Rio Grande
191
Puerto Rico
51
El Yunque
Playa Fajardo
Naval Base

airport
capital
city of interest
city/town
mountains

Event: It's a three-foot-tall eating machine with kangaroo legs and vampire fangs; it lives off the fresh blood of any living creature and is known as "The Goat-sucker." And it stalks the shadows of Puerto Rico. Sightings of *El Chupacabras* were first reported in early 1995; since then, thousands of animals have fallen victim to its alien thirst for blood.

Being there: Ufologists heading for Puerto Rico will be most interested in hiking trips to the national forest, El Yunque, where many UFO reports originate. Also of interest is the town of Canovanas, where *El Chupacabras* was first encountered.

Accommodation

Puerto Rico has no shortage of accommodation, ranging from strictly low-budget to five-star hotels. However, accommodation in the smaller towns, such as Canovanas, can be basic.

Useful Contacts

Puerto Rico Tourism Company
2 La Princesa Drive
Box 4435
Old San Juan Station
San Juan
Puerto Rico 00905   Tel. +1-787-721-2400

Bahia Salinas Beach Hotel
Route 301
Cabo Rojo
Puerto Rico 00622
Tel. +1-787-254-1212   Fax. +1-787-254-1215

El Centro Hotel
Medical Centre,
Rio Piedras
San Juan
Puerto Rico 00926   Tel. +1-787-751-1335

"Welcome to Puerto Rico Program"
Tel. +1-787-791-1014

ABOVE: *When hunting El Chupacabras, be prepared, advise British cryptozoologists Jon Downes and Graham Inglis, who hunted for the alien beast in 1998.*

Location: *Varginha, Minas Gerais region, Brazil*

How to get there: *International flights to São Paulo Airport. Northeast by road to Varginha.*

Event: In the early hours of January 20, 1996, farm workers witnessed the landing of a UFO outside the city of Varginha. Another man, Carlos de Souza, also claims to have watched the craft fall from the sky, and says that, when he approached the crash site, thirty to forty military personnel were already there and had cordoned off the area.

Later that day, three girls walking through the Jardim Andere district witnessed a strange creature trying to hide itself in foliage in Benevenuto Bras Vieira Street. They reported that it had brown-gray skin, red eyes, and three horns sticking out of its head. "It was not animal or human," said one of the girls.

Within a month of these events, a military policeman fell ill with a mysterious multiple infection. Some thirteen days later, he was dead. It later transpired that he had actually been part of a covert operation to capture two aliens. What's more, one or more might still be on the loose ...

Being there: Varginha is a modern Roswell, what with its crashed UFO, military cover-up, alien autopsies, and mysterious deaths. Indeed, Brazil, with its strong paranormal, religious, and alternative cultures, is one of the hottest UFO spots in the world, being home to alien experiencers such as José Higgins, Antonia Villas-Boas, and José Antonio de Silva.

It may take years for the truth to emerge, but the residents are convinced of the ETH. In a recent poll, over eighty percent stated that they believed that an alien spaceship crashed in the region.

Accommodation
There is a wide selection of hotels, lodges, and inns for all pockets and tastes.

Useful contacts
Urupes Park Hotel
(Jardim Andere district)
Tel. +55-35-214-1511
Fax +55-35-214-1414

Jaraguá Hotel
Tel./Fax. +55-35-221-3133

Fenicia Palace
Tel. +55-35-222-3000

Varginha Hotline
If you see the creature itself, report your sighting to the local hotline on:
+55-35-222-1020

Location: *Mexico City, Mexico*

How to get there: *International flights to Mexico City Airport*

Event: During the solar eclipse on July 11, 1991, thousands of witnesses saw a shiny, disk shape pass in front of the sun. Video evidence analysis showed it to be a metallic object, spinning on its axis. UFOs have continued to buzz Mexico City, and thousands of hours of video footage have been obtained. Sightings peak on September 16, (Independence Day).

Being there: In 1993, ufologists descended on the capital for skywatching and remote-viewing and claimed great success when they were buzzed by a few "other-worldly" craft.

ABOVE: *As the world's largest metropolis, Mexico City is as good a choice as any for aliens to reconnoiter. But how long will it take for them to make their agenda known?*

Accommodation

There is no shortage of accommodation, for all budgets.

Useful contacts

Mexico City Tourist Center
Tel. +52-5-250-8555

J. R. Plaza Aeropuerto
Boulevard Aeropuerto 380
Moctezuma Segunda Seccion
Mexico City, Distrito Federal
15530
Tel. +52-5-785-5318

Hotel San Martin
Eje Central Lazaro Cardenas 84
Centro
Mexico City, Distrito Federal
6010
Tel. +52-5-529-6628
Fax. +52-5-529-6788

Hertz Latino Car Hire
Versalles 6
Juarez
Mexico City, Distrito Federal
6680
Tel. +52-5-592-2869

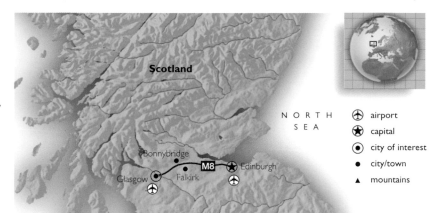

Location:
*Bonnybridge, Stirlingshire,
Scotland*

How to get there:
*International flights to
Glasgow; M8 east to
Bonnybridge*

Event: About one-tenth of the population of this town have reported UFO activity—disks, triangles, and a huge craft shaped like a Toblerone chocolate bar. In 1996, local official William Buchanan had an experience during which he was "told" that the "Council of Nine" Guardians of the Universe was monitoring Bonnybridge.

Being There: Bonnybridge is Britain's Roswell with Hessdalen's weather. The sheer volume of reported sightings suggests that you should see something during a visit—but do so during the summer, when there's a chance of decent weather. The sightings seem to peak at the weekend.

ABOVE: *Bonnybridge, in central Scotland, is Britain's prime UFO hotspot. According to local official Buchanan, there have even been plans drawn up for a UFO theme park "to rival Disneyland."*

Accommodation

You can count the number of hotels in Bonnybridge on one hand, and many visitors choose to stay in nearby Falkirk, the former northernmost frontier of the Roman Empire. This is a good base for visiting local attractions, such as the Polmonthill Ski Centre and any of the five golf courses. Glasgow and Edinburgh are also within half an hour's drive.

Useful Contacts

*Falkirk Tourist
Information Centre
2/4 Glebe Street
Falkirk
Tel. 01324 620244*

*Polmonthill Ski Centre
Tel. 01324 503835*

*Golfing in the area
Tel. 01324 506176*

*Falkirk Town Hall
West Bridge Street
Falkirk
Tel. 01324 506192*

*Bonnybridge Public
Library
Bridge Street
Bonnybridge*

Tel. 01324 503295

*For more information
regarding Bonnybridge,
contact:*

*Strange Phenomenon
Investigations
96 Sherrifspark
Linlithgow
West Lothian
Scotland EH49 7SS
Tel. 01506 845152*

*BUFORA LTD (British UFO
Research Association)
16 Southway
Burgess Hill
Sussex RH15 9ST*

Location: *Nullarbor Plain, southern coast of Australia*

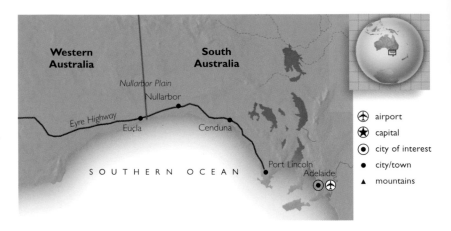

Western Australia

South Australia

Nullarbor Plain
Nullarbor

Eyre Highway
Eucla
Cenduna

SOUTHERN OCEAN

Port Lincoln
Adelaide

⊕ airport
★ capital
◉ city of interest
● city/town
▲ mountains

How to get there: *International flights to Perth Airport, then travel by road along the Eyre Highway, the longest, straightest road in the world.*

Event: On January 20, 1988, the Knowles family had a bizarre UFO encounter while driving across the Nullarbor Plain. The object picked their car off the ground before dropping to earth. The family escaped, hiding in bushes until the object departed. Samples of a mysterious powder taken from the car by police for analysis revealed traces of an astatine isotope that has a very short half-life.

Being there: Nullarbor, which takes it names from the Latin for "no trees," is fairly devoid of life. There are limited facilities across the Plain, so make sure you always have more than enough water.

Accommodation
The Nullarbor Plain is a desolate area, and although there is accommodation at most of the major stop-offs, make sure you plan your journey thoroughly.

Useful Contacts
Nullarbor Traveller (Camping tours of Nullarbor Plain)
P.O. Box 72
Glenside
Adelaide
South Australia 5065
Tel. +61 8 8364 0407   Fax. +61 8 8364 0410

Nullarbor Hotel
Eyre Highway
Nullarbor
South Australia
Tel. +61 8 8625 6271

Ceduna Airport Caravan Park
Highway One
Ceduna
South Australia 5690
Tel. +61 8 8625 2416   Fax. +61 8 8625 2416

Ceduna Caravan & Tourist Centre
29 McKenzie Street
Ceduna
South Australia 5690
Tel. +61 8 8625 2150

ABOVE: *The Eyre Highway, the straightest road in the world, cuts through the Nullarbor Plain. Here, Faye Knowles and her family had a UFO encounter that remains unexplained.*

Location:
Bass Strait, near Cape
Otway, Australia

**How to get
there:**
International flights
into Melbourne;
domestic flights to
King Island.

airport
capital
city of interest
city/town
mountains

Event: On October 21, 1978, flying instructor Frederick Valentich was flying over the Bass Straits when he radioed this message to Melbourne Air Traffic Control: "Four bright ... Seems to me like landing lights ... Just passed over me ... at least 1,000 feet above ... It's approaching now from due east, towards me ... He's flying over me ... It's not an aircraft, it's ... It's a long shape ... Cannot identify ... It's got a green light and a sort of metallic like ... It's all shiny on the outside."

Valentich then said that he would make it to King Island before calling out: "It's hovering on top of me again ... It's hovering and it's not an aircraft." There was a cry, followed by a metallic grinding noise, then nothing. Despite several days of extensive search, no trace of Valentich or his Cessna was ever seen again.

Being there: The Bass Strait is one of the busiest UFO hotspots, but there is no shortage of other things to see and do. The mainland coast is nicknamed "The Wildlife Coast" because of its marine and coastal parks. Follow the coast from Philip Island, with its penguin parade and seal rocks, to reach Wilson's Prom, The Ninety-Mile Beach, and the Lakes National Park.

Accommodation
There is no need to worry about accommodation around the Bass Strait since the whole area caters for tourism. Choice ranges from package-deal resorts to secluded hillside retreats.

Useful Contacts
*South Gippsland Visitor Information Centre
Corner South Gippsland Highway & Silkstone Road
Korumburra 3950
Victoria
Tel. +61 3 5655 2233   Fax. +61 3 5658 1233*

*Philip Island Information Centre
Philip Island Tourist Road
Newhaven 3925
Victoria
Tel. +61 3 5956 7447   Fax. +61 3 5956 7095*

*Cowes Caravan Park
Victoria
Tel. +61 3 5952 2211*

*Kaloha Holiday Resort
Chapel Street
Cowes 3992
Victoria
Tel. +61 3 5952 2179
Fax. +61 3 5952 2723*

UFO REPORT FORM

CASE NUMBER: _____

WITNESS DETAILS

Full Name Mr/Mrs/Miss/Ms...

....

Address..

.... Zip Code...............

Telephone...

Occupation...

SIGHTING DETAILS

Date.........................Time...............................

Duration..

How did you know the time and duration of the sighting

(e.g. wristwatch) ....

Where were you when you saw the object?

Nearest postal address..

....

Additional location details...

....

What were you doing at the time you saw the object, and

how did you happen to notice it?................................

....

....

If you saw the object during daylight, twilight, or dawn,
where was the sun when you observed the object?

(Circle one)

a. in front of you   b. behind you   c. to your right

d. To your left   e. overhead   f. don't remember

If you saw the object at night, twilight, or dawn, what
did you notice concerning the stars?

STARS *(Circle one)*

a. None

b. A few

c. Many

d. Don't remember

MOON *(Circle one)*

a. Bright moonlight

b. Dull moonlight

c. No moonlight

d. Don't remember

Was the object brighter than the background of the sky?

(Circle one)   a. Yes   b. No   c. Don't remember

WEATHER CONDITIONS

What were the weather conditions at the time you saw
the object?

CLOUDS *(Circle one)*

a. Clear sky

b. Hazy

c. Scattered Clouds

d. Thick clouds

e. Don't remember

WIND *(Circle one)*

a. No wind

b. Slight breeze

c. Strong winds

d. Don't remember

PRECIPITATION *(Circle one)*

a. Dry

b. Fog, mist or light rain

c. Moderate or heavy rain

d. Snow

e. Don't remember

TEMPERATURE *(Circle one)*

a. Cold

b. Cool

c. Warm

d. Hot

e. Don't remember

OBJECT

If there was more than one object, how many were there?

....

....

....

....

CASE NUMBER: _____

OBJECT Continued

Draw a picture of how they were arranged, and add an arrow to show the direction in which they were traveling.

Draw a picture that shows the motion of the object(s). Place an "A" at the beginning of the path, and a "B" at end. Note any changes in direction during the course.

How large did the object(s) appear as compared with one of the following objects held in the hand and at arm's length?

(Circle one)

a. Head of a pin
b. Pen
c. Small coin
d. Large coin
e. Golf ball
f. Apple
g. Grapefruit
h. Football
i. Other

If possible, try to estimate what the actual size of the object was in its longest dimension ....
....
....

The edges of the object were:

(Circle one)

a. Fuzzy
b. Like a bright star
c. Sharp outlines
d. Don't remember

Did the object:

(Circle one response in each case)

a. Appear to stand still at any time? Yes No Don't know
b. Suddenly speed up and rush away at any time? Yes No Don't know
c. Break up into parts or explode? Yes No Don't know
d. Give off smoke? Yes No Don't know
e. Change brightness? Yes No Don't know
f. Change shape? Yes No Don't know
g. Flicker, throb, or pulsate? Yes No Don't know

Did the object appear:

(Circle one)

a. Solid
b. Transparent
c. Don't know

Do you think you can estimate the speed of the object?

(Circle one)   a. Yes   b. No

If YES, please estimate the speed ....
....

Do you think you can estimate how far you were from the object?

(Circle one)   a. Yes   b. No

If YES, please estimate the distance ....
....

CASE NUMBER: _____

Place an "A" on the curved line to show how high the object was when you first saw it.

overhead

horizon

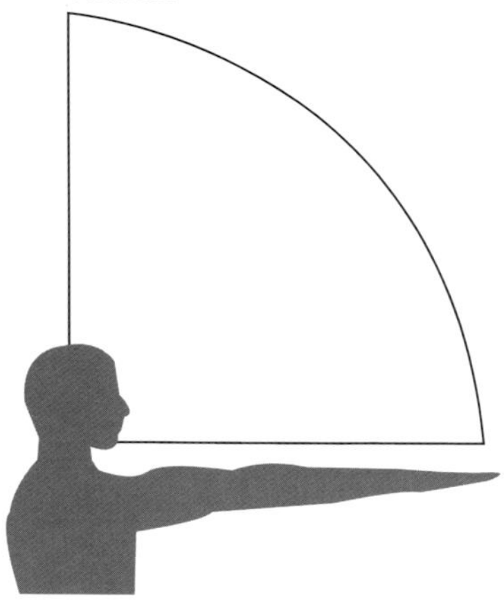

Place an "A" at the position the object was when you first saw it, and "B" where you last saw it.

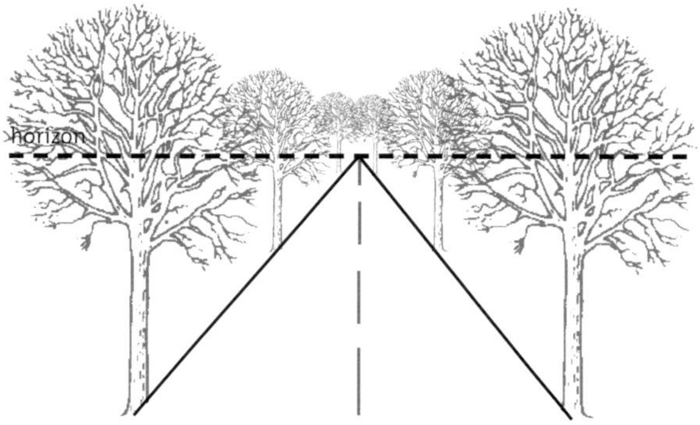

horizon

Was anyone else with you at the time you saw the object?	*(Circle one)*	a. Yes	b. No
If YES, did they see the object(s), too?	*(Circle one)*	a. Yes	b. No

Please list their names, addresses, and telephone numbers below:

....

....

....

....

....

....

On the reverse of this sheet, write a description of the event you observed. You may repeat information already given in the questionnaire, or add further comments. Please try to present information in the order in which events occurred. Also, please make any additional sketch of what you saw, and add any details such as trees, buildings, landscapes, and people.

Name .... Signature .... Date ....

Useful contacts

UFO GROUPS AND ORGANIZATIONS

These organizations can also put you in contact with smaller local societies.

BRITAIN

Anomalous Phenomena Research Association (APRA)
P.O. Box 21876
London SW6 3WL

British UFO Research Association (BUFORA)
BM BUFORA
London WC1N 3XX

Quest International
Wharfebank House
Wharfebank Business Centre
Ilkley Road
Otley LS21 3JD

Strange Phenomena Investigations (SPI), England
41 Castlebar Road
London W5 2DJ

Strange Phenomena Investigations (SPI), Scotland
96 Sherrifspark
Linlithgow
West Lothian
Scotland EH49 7SS

UK UFO Network
6 Aspbury Croft
Castle Bromwich
Birmingham B36 9TD

U.S.A.

Citizens Against UFO Secrecy (CAUS)
P.O. Box 218
Coventry
CT 06238

Center for the Study of Extraterrestrial Intelligence (CSETI)
P.O. Box 15401
Asheville
NC 28813

Committee for the Scientific Investigation of Claims of the Paranormal (CSICOP)
P.O. Box 703
Amherst
NY 14266

Fund for UFO Research (FUFOR)
P.O. Box 277
Mount Rainier
MD 20712

J. Allen Hynek Center for UFO Studies (CUFOS)
2457 West Peterson Avenue
Chicago
IL 60659

Mutual UFO Network (MUFON)
103 Oldtown Road
Seguin
TX 78155-4099

Stargate International
P.O. Box 85159
Tuscon
AZ 85754-5159

AUSTRALIA

Independent UFO Research
Box 783, Kogarah
N.S.W. 2217

Mutual UFO Network (MUFON)
P.O. Box 27117
Mount Roskill
Auckland 1030

Tasmanian UFO Investigation Centre (TUFOIC)
Box 174
South Hobart
Tasmania 7004

Victorian UFO Research Society (VUFORS)
Box 43
Moorabbin
Victoria 3189

Also, for an academic perspective:

UK
UFO Studies
Department of Psychology
Totton College
Water Lane
Totton
Southampton
SO40 32X
Tel. +44 (0)1703 874874
This department provides a qualification in ufology, by correspondence; it is a unit within the University's psychology course, but is open to anyone.

METEOROLOGICAL SOCIETIES

These bodies will be able to give you details of regional offices and provide detailed weather charts for any requested date. When you are research-ing a case, get the weather report from the weather service in order to eliminate the various meteorological phenomena detailed in this book. Addresses begin on the next page.

BRITAIN
British Meteorological Office
London Road
Bracknell
Berkshire RG12 2SZ

U.S.A.
American Meteorological Society
45 Beacon Street
Boston
MAL 02108-36993

AUSTRALIA
**Australian Meteorological Research
Centre**
GPO Box 1289
Melbourne
Victoria

ASTRONOMICAL ASSOCIATIONS AND OBSERVATORIES

BRITAIN
British Astronomical Association
Burlington House
Piccadilly
London W1V 9AG
Tel. +44 (0) 207 734 4145
Fax. +44 (0) 207 439 4629

Royal Observatory
Blackford Hill
Edinburgh EH9 3HJ

Royal Observatory
Greenwich Hill
Greenwich
London

U.S.A.
American Astronomical Society
2000 Florida Avenue
Suite 4000
Washington
DC 20009
Tel. +1-202-328-2010
Fax. +1-202-234-2560

**Goddard Institute for Space
Studies**
NASA
Armstrong Hall
2880 Broadway
New York
NY 10025
Tel. +1-212-678-5500
Fax. +1-212-678-5552

National Solar Observatory
Sacramento Peak
Sunspot
NM

Palomar Observatory
County Road, S6
Pasadena
CA

AUSTRALIA
**Astronomical Society of
Australia**
(contact J. W. O'Byrne, Secretary)
School of Physics
University of Sydney
N.S.W. 2006
Tel. +61 2 9351 3184
Fax. +61 2 9351 7726

Anglo-Australian Observatory
P.O. Box 296
Epping
New South Wales 1710

Sydney Observatory
Watson Road
Observatory Hill
The Rocks
N.S.W.

Perth Observatory
Walnut Road
Bickely
Western Australia 6076

AVIATION AUTHORITIES
(See top of next column)

BRITAIN
Civil Aviation Authority
CAA House
45–59 Kingsway
London WC2B 6TE

U.S.A.
Federal Aviation Administration
800 Independence Avenue
Room 905
Washington DC 20591

AUSTRALIA
Australian Federation of Air Pilots
132 Albert Road
South Melbourne
Victoria 3025

GEOLOGICAL SOCIETIES

BRITAIN
The British Geological Society
Burlington House
Piccadilly
London W1V OJU

U.S.A.
Geological Society of America
P.O. Box 9140
Boulder
CO 80301–9140

AUSTRALIA
**The Geological Society of
Australia**
706 Wynward House
301 George Street
Sydney
N.S.W.

CROP RESEARCH CENTRES

BRITAIN
The Soil Association
86 Colston St.
Bristol, BS1 5BB
Tel. +44 (0)117 929 0661
Fax. +44 (0)117 925 2504

Institute of Arable Crops (IACR)
Rothamstead
Harpenden
Herts AL5 25Q
Tel. +44 (0)1582 763133
Fax. +44 (0)1582 760981

U.S.A.
Department of Agriculture
Agriculture Research Service
Research Laboratory
3420 NW Orchard Ave.
Corvallis
OR 97330

AUSTRALIA
Crop and food research
P.O. Box 1282
Albury
N.S.W. 2640
Tel./fax. T. Stratton on
+61 2 6021 4230

VETERINARY
ORGANIZATIONS

BRITAIN
Royal College of Veterinary Surgeons
Belgravia House
62 Horseferry Road
London SW1P
tel: +44 (0)207 222 2001

U.S.A.
American Veterinary Medical Association
1931 North Meacham Rd.
Suite 100
Schaumburg
IL 60173
Tel. +1-847-925-8070
Fax. +1-847-925-1329

AUSTRALIA
Australian Veterinary Association
AVA House
134 Hampden Rd.
Artamon

N.S.W. 2064
Tel. +61 2 9411 2733
Fax. +61 2 9411 5069

ABDUCTION THERAPY AND
COUNSELING SERVICES

U.S.A.
Intruders Foundation
Budd Hopkins
P.O. Box 30233
New York
NY 10011
Tel. +1-212-645-5278

Academy of Clinical Close Encounter Therapists
2826 O Street
Suite 3
Sacramento
CA 95816

Abductees Anonymous
266 West El Paso Avenue
Clovis
CA 93611–7119

AUSTRALIA
Australian UFO Abduction Study Centre
GPO 1894
Adelaide
South Australia 5001

PSYCHIATRIC SOCIETIES

BRITAIN
British Medical Association
BMA House
Tavistock Square
London WC1H 9JP
tel: +44 (0)207 387 4499

USA
International Center for Mental Health
Mount Sinai School of Medicine
5th Ave. & 100th St.

Box 1093, New York NY
Tel. +1-212-241-6133

Florida Psychiatric Society
521 East Park Ave.
Tallahassee
FL 32301-2524
Tel. +1-850-222-8404
Fax. +1-850-224-8406

AUSTRALIA
The Royal Australia & N.Z. College of Psychiatry
309 La Trobe Street
Melbourne
Victoria 3000
Tel. +61 3 9640 0646
Fax. +61 3 9642 5652

HYPNOTHERAPY
ORGANIZATIONS

BRITAIN
British Hypnotherapy Association
67 Upper Berkeley Street
London W1H 7DH
Tel: + 44 (0)207 723 4443

National Association of Counsellors, Hypnotherapists and Psychotherapists
Ffynnonwen
Llangwryryfon
Aberystwyth
Dyfed SY23 4EY
Wales
Tel./Fax. +44 (0)1974 241376

U.S.A.
World Board of Hypnotherapy Education
1555 East Flamingo Road
Suite 330
Las Vegas
NV 89119

AUSTRALIA
Cronulla & Sutherland

Hypnotherapy
7 Chamberlain Avenue
Carringbah
Sydney
N.S.W. 2229
Tel. +61 2 9225 9911

FOLKLORE SOCIETIES

U.S.A.
**Folklore Society of Greater
Washington**
P.O. Box 5693
Friendship Heights Station
Washington
DC 200016–2228
Tel. +1-202-546-2228

New York Folklore Society
632 W. Buffalo St
Ithaca
NY 14850
Tel. +1-607-273-9137
Fax. +1-607-273-3620

"REMOTE VIEWING"
[PSYCHIC SPYING]

BRITAIN
Paranormal Management Systems
P.O. Box 2749
Brighton BN2 2DR
Tel. +44 (0)1273 690424

U.S.A.
The Psychic Learning Center
Benson Wong
3754 Sacramento Street
San Francisco
CA 94118

PHOTOGRAPHIC ANALYSIS
*As with physical evidence, photo-
graphic evidence should, ideally, be
assessed by professionals. There are
few facilities around for such analysis, and they are usually very expen-*
*sive. So, if you do decide to use them,
try to make sure your material has
already been through as many stages
as possible before you hand it over to
the professional analysts. The alternative is to work in collaboration
with a national UFO group (listed
earlier), which might be interested in
financing the analysis, although
these groups may wish to take over
the investigation of the entire case.*

BRITAIN
Faculty of Engineering
(contact Dr. Roger Green)
University of Bradford
Richmond Road
Bradford BD7 1DP
Tel. +44 (0)1274 234007
Fax. +44 (0)1274 234727

Quest International
(contact Russel Callaghan)
Wharfebank House
Wharfebank Business Centre
Ilkley Road
Otley LS21 3JD

U.S.A.
MUFON Staff Photoanalyst
(contact Jeff Sainio)
2200 Good Hope Road, No. 321
Glendale
WI 53209-2763
Tel. +1-414-246-7829/315-0795

Eastman Kodak
343 State Street
Rochester
NY 14650-0315
Tel. +1-716-724-4000

AUSTRALIA
Imaging Investigation
Level 6, 440 Elizabeth Street
Melbourne
Tel. +61 3 9925 5334
Fax. +61 3 9925 5372

RESEARCH
*Most of the following are Freedom of
Information Act offices that you can
write to requesting details on any
aspect of the UFO phenomenon. In
each instance, head the address with
"FOIA/PA Unit." The alternative is to
scour national archives, also listed –
and on personal visits, make sure you
go armed with proof of identity, pencil and notebook, money/credit card
(for buying documents), and loose
change for photocopiers and lockers.*

BRITAIN
Public Records Office
Ruskin Avenue
Kew
Richmond
Surrey TW9 4DU

U.S.A.
FBI Headquarters
J. Edgar Hoover Building
Washington DC 20535
Tel. +1-202-324-5520
*(For FBI information, write to head-
quarters and send a copy of the
request to the FBI field office nearest
the incident you are researching. For
details of field offices, call or write to
the headquarters.)*

Central Intelligence Agency
Information and Privacy Coordinator
Central Intelligence Agency
Washington, D.C. 20505
Tel. +1-202-351-5659

**Department of Defense
Headquarters, USAF/DADF**
Washington DC 20330-5025
Tel. +1-202-697-3467

U.S. National Archives
*The U.S. National Archives and
Records Administration (N.A.R.A.) is a
federal agency established in 1934 to*

manage all records pertaining to U.S. history. Individuals over the age of 16 can inspect more than four billion pieces of paper at the 33 N.A.R.A. facilities throughout the country. Also stored are motion picture reels, sound recordings, and photographs. There are two main facilities:

National Archives and Records Administration
National Archives Building
7th Street and Pennsylvania Avenue, N.W.
Washington
DC 20408
Tel. +1-202-501-5400

N.A.R.A.
National Archives at College Park
8601 Adelphi Road
College Park
MD 20740–6001
Tel. +1-301-713-6800

AUSTRALIA
Australian National Archives
Australia's national archives store more than 100 million Common-wealth government records. Records over 30 years old are available to the public under the 1983 Archives Act. There are two main facilities:
Queen Victoria Terrace
Parkes
Canberra
Australia Capital Territories 2600
Tel. +61 2 6212 3900
Fax. +61 2 6212 3999

120 Miller Road
Chester Hill
Sydney
N.S.W. 2162
Tel. +61 2 9645 0110
Fax. +61 2 9645 0108

CONFERENCES
Most of the major UFO groups (see above) hold annual conventions and conferences. For details of specific events, contact the society directly. Other major UFO events organizers include:

BRITAIN
Quest International
For details of Quest conferences, contact:
Lloyds Bank Chambers
West Street
Ilkley LS29 9DW

U.S.A.
International MUFON Symposium
For details, contact:
Mutual UFO Network
103 Oldtowne Road
Seguin
TX 78155–4099
Tel. +1-512-379-9216

Annual International UFO Congress Convention and Film Festival,
Laughlin, NV
For details, contact:
9975 Wadsworth Parkway
#K2-274
Westminster
CO 80021
Tel. +1-303-643-9443
Fax. +1-303-543-8667

Project Awareness Gulf Breeze UFO Conference
For details, contact:
Lucius Farish
2 Caney Valley Drive
Plumerville
AZ 72127-8725
Tel. +1-501-354-2558

Reading and references

Abducted, Ann Andrews, Jean Ritchie, Headline, London, 1998

Alien Base, Timothy Good, Century, London, 1998

Alien Encounters, David M. Jacobs, Virgin, London, 1994

An Alien Harvest, Linda Moulton Howe, Linda Moulton Howe Productions, Pennsylvania, 1989

Alien Liaison, Timothy Good, Arrow Books, London, 1992

"Attack of the Chupacabras,", Tim Coleman, *The X Factor* partwork magazine, No 18, pp.477–481

"The Aviary," Peter Brookesmith, *The X Factor* partwork magazine, No. 15, pp.393–97

Beyond Roswell, Michael Hesemann & Philip Mantle, Michael O'Mara Books, London, 1997

Beyond Top Secret, Timothy Good, Sidgwick & Jackson, London, 1996

"Caught on Camera," Tim Coleman, *The X Factor* partwork magazine, No.35, pp.967–971

The Coming of the Saucers, Kenneth Arnold, Ray Palmer, private publication, Amherst, 1952

Confrontation, Jacques Vallee, Ballantine Books, New York, 1990

"Conspiracy Researcher," Craig Glenday, *The X Factor* partwork magazine, No.8, pp.213–215

A Covert Agenda, Nick Redfern, Simon & Schuster, London, 1997

Crash at Corona, Stanton T. Friedman, Marlowe & Co., New York, 1995

Faces of the Visitors, Kevin Randle, Russ Estes, Fireside, New York, 1997

The Field Guide to Extraterrestrials, Patrick Huyghe, New English Library, London, 1997

Fire in the Sky, Travis Walton, Marlow & Co., New York, 1979

Flying Saucers Have Landed (rev.), Desmond Leslie & George Adamski, Neville Spearman, London, 1970

Forensic Science Handbook, Richard Saferstein (ed.), Prentice-Hall, New Jersey [date unknown, internet version]

From Outer Space to You, Howard Menger, Saucerian, Clarksburg, 1959

Glimpses of Other Realities: Volume One: Facts and Eyewitnesses, Linda Moulton Howe, Linda Moulton Howe Productions, Pennsylvania, 1993

The Gulf Breeze Sightings, Edward & Francis Walters, Avon Books, New York, 1990

Heavenly Bodies: A Beginner's Guide to Astronomy, Iain Nicholson, BBC Books, London, 1994

"Hypnosis and UFO abductions: A Troubled Relationship," Alvin Lawson, *Proceedings of the First International UFO Congress*, Warner Books, New York, 1980

Hypnotherapy Resources and Career Guide, Morris L. Berg, Symbolon Press, London, 1998

The Interrupted Journey, John Fuller, Dial Press, New York, 1966

"A Mad Dash of Meteors," Susan C. French, *Skywatch '99*, 1999, pp.76–7

Making Contact, Bill Fawcett (ed.), William Morrow & Co., New York, 1997

MIB: Investigating the Truth Behind The Men In Black Phenomenon, Jenny Randles, Piatkus, London, 1997

"Mind Power," John Shreeve, *The X Factor* partwork magazine, No.31, pp.845–849

Observing UFOs, Richard F. Haines, Nelson Hall, Chicago, 1980

Open Skies, Closed Minds, Nick Pope, Simon & Schuster, London, 1996

The Paranormal: An Illustrated Encyclopedia, Stuart Gordon, Headline, London, 1992

Passport to Magonia, Jacques Vallee, Henry Regnery, Chicago, 1969

Philip's Guide to Stars and Planets, Patrick Moore, George Philip Ltd, London, 1993

Physical Trace Cases Associated with UFO Sightings, A Preliminary Catalogue, Ted Phillips, CUFOS, Chicago, 1975

Scientific Examination of Questioned Documents, Hilton Ordway, Elsevier, New York [date unknown, internet version]

"Scientific panel concludes some UFO evidence worthy of study,", David F. Salisbury, *Stanford News*, California, 1998. Full text available on: http://www/jse.com/ufo_reports/Sturrock/toc.html

"Shooting UFOs," Jenny Randles, *The X Factor* partwork magazine, No.5, pp.123–127

"Socorro Case," Patrick Huyghe, unpublished article for *UFO Casebook*, Marshall Cavendish, London, 1998

Spirit Releasement Therapy, William J. Baldwin, Headline Books, Terra Alta, 1992

Statement on Unidentified Flying Objects, James E. McDonald, House Committee on Science and Astronautics, Washington, 1968

Strange Stories of UFOs, Len Ortzen, Coronet Books, Sevenoaks, 1979

TOP SECRET/MAJIC, Stanton T. Friedman, Marlowe & Co., New York, 1996

Travels in Dreamland, Phil Patton, Millennium, London, 1997

The UFO Book, Jerome Clarke, Visible Ink Press, Detroit, 1998

The UFO Cover-up, Lawrence Fawcett, Barry J. Greenwood, Fireside, New York, 1984

The UFO Encyclopaedia, John Spencer, Headline, London, 1997

"UFO Flaps," Martin Kottmeyer, *The Anomalist*, Winter 1995–96, pp.64–87

UFO: Flying Saucers Over Britain?, Robert Chapman, Mayflower, St Albans, 1969

UFO: The Complete Sightings, Peter Brookesmith, Barnes & Noble, New York, 1995

The UFO Handbook, Allan Hendry, Sphere Books, London, 1980

The UFO Mystery, Hilary Evans, Dennis Stacy (eds), John Brown Publishing, London, 1998

UFOs: The Public Deceived, Philip J. Klass, Prometheus Books, New York, 1983

UFOs are Real: Here's the Proof, Edward Walters, Bruce Maccabbee, Avon Books, New York, 1997

The Unexplained, John Spencer, Simon & Schuster, London, 1997

Using the Freedom of Information Act, Fund for Open Information and Accountability, New York

Vital Signs, Andy Thomas, S. B. Publications, Seaford, East Sussex, 1998

The White Sands Incident, Daniel Fry, New Age, Los Angeles, 1954

The World Atlas of UFOs, John Spencer, Smithmark, New York, 1992

The X Files Book of the Unexplained, Volume 1, Jane Goldman, Simon & Schuster, London, 1995

Index

Acknowledgments

AUTHOR'S ACKNOWLEDGMENTS

My sincerest thanks go to everyone who has helped in the creation of this book, and in particular Graham Birdsall and *UFO Magazine*, Professor Leon Brenig, Jerome Clark, Tim Coleman, Paul Devereux, Jon Downes and the Exeter Stange Group, Mary Finney and the Pendleton (Ohio) Public Library, Mike Flynn, Chris Fowler, Freddie, Juventino Garcia, Timothy Good, Nigel Gosden, Roger Green, Linda Moulton Howe, Patrick Huyghe, Dee Johnston, Ann Kay, Jarno Lahtinen, Felix Lejac, Alan Lothian, Kate Matthew at the Expert Witness Institute, everyone at MidsummerBooks who had to put up with disappearing acts, Maxine Pearson, Iain Reid, David Spoor, Edward Steer, Mark Walker ... and The Ship in Wardour Street and the Red Lion in Hoxton Street.

Special thanks go to Stan Friedman for first getting me interested in ufology and honoring me by contributing the foreword, Steve Cook for his stories and alien artwork, Raj Chavda for the best UFO artwork I've seen, and Paul Duncan for the maps and diagrams. Finally, love and thanks to Tom Pearson-Adams and Ben Way (sorry about the front room) for their invaluable help and support.

EDDISON • SADD EDITIONS

Commissioning Editor	Liz Wheeler
Project Editor	Ann Kay
American Editor	Maggi McCormick
Indexer	Dorothy Frame
Art Director	Elaine Partington
Senior Art Editor	Pritty Ramjee
Senior Designer	Marissa Feind
Production	Karyn Claridge, Charles James